THE GREAT
UNCROWNED

THE GREAT
UNCROWNED

FOOTBALL'S MOST
CELEBRATED LOSERS

NEIL FREDRIK JENSEN

First published by Pitch Publishing, 2022

Pitch Publishing
9 Donnington Park,
85 Birdham Road,
Chichester,
West Sussex,
PO20 7AJ
www.pitchpublishing.co.uk
info@pitchpublishing.co.uk

A CIP catalogue record is available for this book
from the British Library.

ISBN 978 1 80150 177 4

Typesetting and origination by Pitch Publishing
Printed and bound in Great Britain by TJ Books Ltd

Contents

The author: Neil Fredrik Jensen

Neil Jensen is a football and business writer who was previously editorial director with a major European investment bank. Neil has been a magazine and website editor, speech-writer and advertising copywriter. He is a member of the Football Writers' Association and the Football Collective, and a Freeman of the City of London. He has written for many publications, including *The Economist*, *The New European*, *World Soccer*, *Football Weekends* and *The Blizzard*. He has also written on football finance for Brand Finance, World Football Summit and Soccerex, among others. A Chelsea supporter since 1967, he now considers himself a portfolio fan and follows a range of clubs, including FC København and Hitchin Town. He is also the creator and editor of the award-winning website, Game of the People.

Dedicated to Carter Jensen,
our little lad in Yokohama, a
child of the pandemic.

1

No disgrace in almost being champions

IN 1974, I predicted the Netherlands would win the World Cup in Germany. It wasn't a brave forecast in my opinion; I had watched Ajax Amsterdam win three consecutive European Cups, delighted in the way they played and even persuaded my mother to doctor a white football shirt with a red band to create an improvised Ajax top. I wanted the Dutch to win the competition because I felt they represented the future of football, a game I had lived and breathed for most of my life. When Johan Cruyff and his pals were beaten 2-1 by West Germany in the final in Munich, I was devastated and felt the football-watching public had been deprived. I wasn't Dutch, but I was an adopted son of the Netherlands for many years. If countries were clubs, I was a fan.

The Dutch were unlucky – unlucky to come up against the host nation, unlucky to have run out of steam after charming the world in the World Cup, unlucky to have scored early in that final, unlucky to have had the burden of history on their orange-clad shoulders. In any other World Cup, with the possible exception of 1970 in Mexico, they would surely have been worthy winners. This was an exceptional team, a golden generation of players marshalled by one of the most influential figures in 20th-century football, but ultimately, a side that failed when it truly mattered. Four years on the Dutch still had the makings of a great team, but once more they were beaten by the host nation. Although their margin of defeat in the final was two goals in Buenos Aires, they were actually closer to victory than many might recall. If Robbie Rensenbrink's tame prod in the dying seconds of normal time had been an inch or two to the right, Argentina would have been beaten and the Netherlands would have had to work out how to get home in one piece.

Sadly the Dutch dream went unfulfilled across two World Cups; they really were nearly men. Their best was not quite good enough, but nobody would have minded if they had won at least one World Cup, Germans and Argentinians excepted of course. That they managed to reach two consecutive finals – four years apart – says a lot about their underlying quality.

More recently, when Liverpool went through the 2018/19 season losing just one game and finishing just one point behind Manchester City, you could sympathise with Jürgen Klopp and his team for producing a spectacular campaign but still being denied the title by an even more proficient side.

The battle for top spot had produced two teams at the height of their game; City won 32 of their 38 games, Liverpool 30. The Reds were 25 points clear of third-placed Chelsea and their only defeat was on New Year's Day at City's Etihad Stadium. Furthermore, both teams scored goals proficiently and swept up the major trophies. City won all three domestic prizes in England while Liverpool were European champions for the sixth time. It is difficult to call Liverpool unlucky, but it was their misfortune that they came up against an all-conquering Manchester City team.

However, it has to be remembered that Liverpool, themselves, were in that exact position in the late 1970s and

1980s and their machine-like run of success denied some very good teams their moment of triumph, such as Queens Park Rangers in 1976, arguably the most 'continental' of English sides in the 1970s. Although Rangers entertained with their flowing, thoughtful style, there was a sense of the inevitable about Liverpool's eventual victory in 1975/76. They had, after all, been there before, while QPR had a 'team for the moment' that had a limited life span. Three years later, Rangers were relegated to the old Second Division.

Similarly, Ipswich Town under Bobby Robson were frequently in the mix when it came to major silverware, but found that their small-club status prevented a level of sustainability that would guarantee success. Quite simply, a lack of resources, be it squad size or financial clout, has prevented some very good line-ups from become winners rather than unfortunate losers.

Not that this has always consigned smaller clubs to a life in the shadows; Ipswich won the league in 1962, but this was largely attributable to the methods of Alf (later Sir Alf) Ramsey, who took a journeyman team to unprecedented success, overcoming the challenge of the great Tottenham double-winners of 1960/61. The only comparable situation could well be Brian Clough and Nottingham Forest in 1977/78, although Forest did sustain their golden period for a few seasons, while Ipswich were soon back in the second tier of the English game. In both cases, the genius of their respective managers was the catalyst for a period of high achievement. In Ipswich's case, in 1962 they benefitted from being an unknown quantity in what was their first season in the First Division, while Forest's title, while well deserved, also took advantage of changes at Liverpool, notably the transition from Kevin Keegan to Kenny Dalglish. They were soon back in the saddle and more rampant than ever, although for a few years, Forest chased them hard.

In some ways, the tale of Leeds United also owes itself to a lack of strength in depth. Anyone who witnessed the period between 1969 and 1973 will be only too aware of how the Yorkshire club failed at the final hurdle all too frequently. Between 1967/68 and 1973/74 Leeds won six major prizes, but in the period from 1964/65 to 1974/75 they were runners-up or finalists eight times. On three occasions, they finished second in the Football League by the narrowest of margins. There was little doubt that Leeds were the best team unit around at that time, but their trophy haul doesn't necessarily bear that out. Why did they lose out so often?

A psychologist would make a good living out of analysing Leeds, but their high level of intensity and rather insular outlook of us against the world made for a lot of drama. They were a wonderful team, but beyond the first-choice 11 or 12 their resources were certainly stretched. They were also Don Revie's team, so when he went the impetus gradually faded. In truth, Leeds should have been champions half a dozen times in the 1970s, but they created the frenetic cup-tie mentality that seemed to accompany every game and when they lost, their critics rejoiced. They also tried to fight battles on many fronts, exhausting their team physically and mentally. It was no coincidence that when they were champions, in 1969 and 1974, their focus was purely on finishing top rather than winning everything in sight.

Intensity and focus has its place and can certainly be exercised over the course of a World Cup or European Championship campaign, which usually comprises half a dozen or so matches. Even the most limited teams can conjure up the concentration and purpose required to be successful. Likewise, a team can lose its momentum just as easily and become underachievers. In some ways, the Netherlands of 1974 did just that, allowing themselves to forget that possession has to be coupled with goalscoring in a World Cup Final.

The case of the Dutch, along with the Hungarians of 1954 and Brazil in 1982, confirms that losers are not always forgotten. Indeed, there has been a certain amount of romanticisation about teams that have played wonderful football but end up tragic losers. We have learnt that while the best teams will invariably win long-haul league titles, they do not always emerge on top in knockout competitions or high-pressured tournaments. Hence, the Netherlands, Hungary and Brazil have exited World Cups with little reward other than the glowing praise of the public.

In each example, these teams all fell short of expectations because of capitulation in a vital game: the Dutch, as mentioned, took the lead against the West Germans but lost in the 1974 final; Hungary were beaten 3-2 by the Germans after leading 2-0 in Berne 20 years previously; and Brazil's instinct to attack after equalising against Italy saw them surprisingly lose 3-2 in 1982 when they were expected to go on to win the World Cup. All three games are etched in the psyche of football in their respective countries as defining moments when paradise got lost. Human error, concentration and the unpredictable nature of the game made them all into nearly men.

We should not be too surprised that this can happen in football, given the minuscule margins between success and failure. One goal changes the entire outcome of a game; indeed it can alter the end result of an entire season. The FA Cup Final provides a great example of how the fortunes of a team can switch completely by a single goal. Since 1946/47, 48 of the 75 finals have been decided by a margin of one goal, while 24 of these have been 1-0 victories (or defeats). Little wonder that many finals have been tense and often tactically sterile, decided in a split second.

And then there's luck, an element that many coaches have tried to drive out of professional football. 'You make your own luck'; 'the harder I work, the luckier I become'; 'there's no such thing as luck'; these are just some of the ways good old-fashioned 'Lady Luck' has been described. Bad luck in football often manifests itself in the form of an incident that can change a match. Steven Gerrard's notorious fall that let in Demba Ba is still being sung about today, but it was a defining moment in the 2014 season in England and almost certainly deprived Liverpool of the Premier League title. That was certainly bad luck. John Terry's penalty in Moscow, the result of an ill-timed slip, unluckily deprived Chelsea of the Champions League in 2008.

Go back further and the notorious offside decision that never was in 1971 arguably cost Leeds United the championship in a game against West Bromwich Albion, while countless injuries in major games have altered the course of football history. Luck may play a part, but so does cheating and gamesmanship. How else can you describe the famous 'Hand of God' incident in Mexico City in 1986? It was England's misfortune that Diego Maradona got away with blatantly scoring with his hand. That was bad luck for England, but it owed its origins to what many today would call 'shithousery'.

Success can be measured in different ways and is forever relative. Today, it is very difficult to imagine a tiny country being world champions, such as Uruguay in 1930 and 1950, or a small club like Wimbledon winning a major honour. For most, lower-level victories such as promotion would represent the peak of their achievements. In England, 50 per cent of the 92 English Premier League and Football League clubs have won major silverware in some shape or form. Many do not even get close to 'nearly men' status.

Some believe football has become a game of 'winner takes all' and that there are too few moments when clubs can celebrate. Therefore, they argue, we need a system that creates more winners than we currently have. The victors and their spoils are well-televised, garlanded with golden ticker-tape and jets of flame unnecessarily heating the stadium. The scenes are very much a cliché and a statement about the way we see success in the modern age of celebrity.

Today, we almost expect football's top players to be consistently successful because they play for the leading clubs. Consider that Lionel Messi has won 11 league titles and more than 160 caps for Argentina, while his rival, Cristiano Ronaldo, has won seven and almost 200 respectively. Both have played in World Cups but neither have won the competition, yet this has not dulled the lustre of their reputations. George Best, considered one of the all-time greats, won very few honours in his career and played for Northern Ireland on the international stage. He never appeared in the World Cup, like the great Alfredo Di Stéfano, but their place in football's pantheon is secure. You do not have to be a world champion to be remembered.

Thankfully, the game has always acknowledged that it takes two to tango, that we cannot all be winners and there are losers. Glorious losers, unlucky losers, outfought losers and quite simply, second-best losers – football has them all. There are a host of factors why there are achievers and why there are teams that couldn't quite get there. But being number two should not be considered failure, far from it. Why else would we hold teams like Hungary in 1954, QPR of 1976, Brazil in 1982 and Newcastle United's 1996 Premier League challengers in such high esteem? We remember them because they gave us moments to savour and that makes them winners by so many different criteria. If we celebrate those who contributed to making the season so interesting and competitive, we can remove some of the 'win or bust' aspect to football, and that might just make people feel better about not being champions but being very good nearly men.

2

Oldham Athletic 1915:
The forgotten runners-up

THE 1914/15 season in England is really remembered for only one thing: football carried on as the First World War started and soon every high street in Britain was providing evidence of the carnage that became trench warfare. But for every person who wanted football to prevail, there were many more who felt that the continuation of something as frivolous as sport was inappropriate and more than a little unpatriotic.

The Football Association and Football League vowed to provide entertainment and morale-boosting distraction to the population. 'Any national sport which would minimise the grief, help the nation to bear its sorrow, relieve the oppression of continuous strain and save the people from panic and undue depression is a great asset,' said the Football League.

Those who didn't immediately answer the call to arms were often the brunt of fierce criticism. It was not uncommon to see slogans daubed on walls in towns, especially in the north of England, where recruitment drives were in full force: 'Wanted, petticoats for all able-bodied youths who have not yet joined the army.'

The well-known philanthropist and brewer, F.N. Charrington, complained in the press about the decision to maintain regular football, 'The unpatriotic decision of the Football Association has filled me, and doubtless tens of thousands of Britishers, with shame and indignation.'

While many footballers joined the crusade against Kaiser Wilhelm, the Football League got under way and the First Division turned out to be one of the tightest, most intensely contested campaigns of all time.

The public tentatively supported the game, although attendances fell by 38 per cent in 1914/15, plummeting after Christmas when people realised that the war was not ending soon. Some clubs saw their support decline dramatically; Manchester United's attendances dropped by 53.2 per cent, Tottenham 52 per cent, Sunderland 51 per cent, Chelsea 50 per cent and Aston Villa 46 per cent. The decline in gate money had a negative impact on the financial strength of all the major clubs, who were still committed to paying the few professional players who had not enlisted. Little wonder that the Football League declared its clubs were in a 'helpless position'.

This may have contributed to the fall of some of the bigger football institutions in 1914. One of the most unlikely of clubs, Oldham Athletic, almost become Football League champions, only denied at the last hurdle by Everton, who had finished 15th in 1913/14. Newcastle, Sunderland, Aston Villa and Manchester United were not as strong as they had been in the pre-First World War years.

Never have Oldham gone as close to winning the top prize as they did in 1915, even if their attendances at Boundary Park, an average of 9,000, were only half of those enjoyed by nearby Manchester City and were the lowest in the First Division.

Oldham had finished fourth in 1913/14, a respectable position, but this gave little indication of what was to follow in the last full programme for five years. Oldham's manager was the moustachioed David Ashworth, a Blackpool-born referee who was appointed in 1906. In 1914, after taking Oldham into the First Division and up to fourth, he resigned and took a job with Stockport County. Oldham were surprised by Ashworth's departure, but they had 48 applicants for the vacant role. Ashworth went on to win the league title with Liverpool in 1922.

Herbert Bamlett, from the north-east, was Oldham's choice to replace Ashworth, and another highly respected referee. Bamlett, who was only 32, had officiated the 1914 FA Cup Final between Liverpool and Burnley and the Scotland versus England international that year. Oldham was the start of his managerial career; he later led Wigan Borough, Middlesbrough and Manchester United.

With players enlisting in the armed forces, Oldham had little choice but to go with the bulk of their 1913/14 squad, although they paid £100 for Manchester United's 20-year-old forward Arthur Cashmore, who had promise but was very injury-prone. They were keen to persevere with the young striker Arthur Gee, a bustling forward who had shown potential but could be difficult to manage.

The biggest name in the Oldham squad was another former Manchester United man, Charlie Roberts, a strong centre-half who was a leader on the field. Roberts had a chequered career, notably in his role in setting up the Football Players' Union with Billy Meredith in 1907. A burly, well-built man, Roberts was 31, many felt he was a little past his best and his fitness was in question. Nevertheless, his move to Oldham in 1913 was one of the biggest transfers of that summer. Oldham paid £1,500 and Roberts himself received £225, a considerable sum at the time. It was later suggested that he had departed Manchester United because he was refused a second benefit game by the club. More likely, United's refurbishment and expansion of Old Trafford meant they were happy to get some cash for their player.

Roberts was instantly made captain of Oldham and became extremely popular with the club's followers. However, rather than move to the Lancashire mill town, he continued to live in Manchester as he had several business interests in the city, including a large newspaper shop.

Having players like Roberts didn't come cheap and at the end of his first season at Boundary Park, Oldham announced a loss of £1,482 which they blamed on their FA Cup first round exit at Brighton. A year earlier they had reached the semi-final, losing to Aston Villa.

Oldham had also spent £6,000 on their ground, opening a new stand at the start of 1913/14. They had also bought their home for £3,000. Despite the loss, Oldham's directors insisted they were in a sound financial position.

The consensus in the media was that Oldham were a progressive club and their acquisition of Roberts reflected their ambition. One newspaper noted, 'Oldham Athletic are an eloquent example of grit and enterprise, rising superior to adversity.' The only area of the team that didn't win praise was the forward line; hence the signing of Cashmore was designed to solve a problem – in 1913/14, Oldham's 55 league goals was matched by bottom-placed Derby County. Cashmore didn't join the team until November 1914 and in total he made just 16 appearances in 1914/15, scoring eight goals.

Oldham started their league campaign at Old Trafford, home of Manchester United. Four years earlier United had been league champions, but they had only finished 14th in 1913/14. United looked upon Oldham as a relatively small club, so when the Latics came away with a 3-1 win before 15,000 people, it was a surprise result. Arthur Gee, starting the season well, scored two early goals but United responded just before the break. Oldham wrapped things up with a late goal from former Aston Villa inside-forward Joe Walters. Oldham had impressed the watching experts, who felt that their half-back line, ably led by Roberts, would prove to be a 'rare power' in 1914/15.

The strength of Oldham's half-backs was proving to be key to their hopes for the campaign. When they beat Bolton Wanderers a few days later, the robust middle line was too much for the Trotters, who were beaten 5-3 in an exciting game at Boundary Park. All eight goals were scored in a frantic first half.

Oldham lost their unbeaten record at reigning champions Blackburn Rovers but at the end of September 1914 they were nicely placed in third, one point behind The Wednesday – later Sheffield Wednesday – and Manchester City. They had also scored a notable 2-1 victory away at Sunderland's Roker Park, outclassing the home team who struggled to deal with Oldham's 'over-strenuous' style.

The Wednesday, the early leaders, were next at Boundary Park, the biggest game of the league season so far. The sceptics were still ignoring Oldham as potential champions and even though they pulverised Wednesday in the first half, scoring three goals in under 20 minutes and eventually winning 5-2, not everyone was impressed by the way the Latics overpowered their opponents. 'Oldham are a sound side who seem to have decided to throw finesse overboard and go for goal on every conceivable occasion,' read one report.

The league title race had already hinted it was going to be a tight affair, with Manchester City and The Wednesday leading the way and Oldham in hot pursuit. A 3-2 victory at Burnley at the start of November was impressive and after beating Tottenham 4-1, Oldham went to the top of the table. Wednesday beat Manchester City 2-1 in the game of the day, but the anti-football brigade were in full flow, calling for the game to be suspended as the war continued. 'It is much more desirable that professional football players should find employment in His Majesty's forces than in their old profession,' screamed one headline.

Oldham were leading the way for the first time in their history but some members of the press still felt that the team was 'dour and stubborn', even if the players had plenty of 'dash and penetration'. Once again, when they travelled to Newcastle United, a fading force, few experts anticipated an Oldham win, but they were wrong and the Latics went two points clear at the top.

A 5-1 win against Middlesbrough showed that despite the absence of Gee and Walters, Oldham could still score goals; their 36 from 14 games was the best total in the division. Still the press box failed to recognise the quality of the Latics' team, claiming they were not a patch on the past two league champions, Sunderland and Blackburn. However, there was no shortage of stamina in the line-up and in defence, the full-backs, Billy Cook and Jimmy Hodson, were extremely solid, if lacking a little artistry.

But a setback was around the corner for the league leaders in the shape of a three-goal defeat at Sheffield United on an afternoon of high winds and torrential rain. The home side had called Oldham the strongest and most balanced team in the division, but at Bramall Lane they were a shadow of the group who had beaten United's city rivals, Wednesday. Oldham lost the leadership that day but they were back on top a week later, drawing 3-3 at home to Aston Villa, who had to rely on a last-minute goal to earn a point. Manchester City, who had taken over as leaders, were trounced 4-1 by Everton, a rising menace.

Oldham extended their lead at the top to three points and ended 1914 on 29 points from 19 games, three ahead of Manchester City and four in front of Everton, Blackburn and The Wednesday. Many football commentators finally predicted that unfashionable Oldham would win the championship in April.

With so many teams fancying their chances of a championship challenge, big games came almost every weekend. Oldham, on New Year's Day, welcomed Manchester City to Boundary Park. The game, which was ruined by the weather, ended in a draw and then Oldham were beaten at Bolton. They remained top of the table but there was some suggestion, not for the last time, that the players were tiring, and that Oldham's aggressive and powerful style was taking a lot of nervous and physical energy from the squad, particularly older players such as Billy Cook, Charlie Roberts, Ollie Tummon, Jimmy Hodson and Hugh Moffat.

Oldham's challenge did look like it was starting to flounder, though, and a five-game sequence without a victory was very damaging. They ended January with a 2-1 defeat at Notts County and then took part in a remarkable game at home to Sunderland. The Wearsiders won 5-4 and were in control for most of the match, which was played on a sand-covered pitch. This defeat raised questions about Oldham's ability to last the pace and over the coming weeks, the answer became quite evident. By the end of February they were top again, but the title race was becoming very claustrophobic with only four points separating the top eight clubs.

Oldham slipped up at home to West Bromwich Albion which meant that The Wednesday were now the leaders, but a 4-3 victory at Everton rekindled hopes that the Latics could still be champions. The victory came at a cost, though, for Scottish international winger Joe Donnachie was injured and didn't play again for the rest of the season.

Successive defeats at Tottenham and Bradford City suggested Oldham were drifting out of contention, but such was the inconsistency of their rivals they were one of four teams on 37 points, all of whom were just one point behind leaders Manchester City. It was anyone's prize in 1914/15.

The contenders did their best to compromise their own bids for glory. City, for example, won just one of their last six games, including a goalless draw with Oldham.

The Latics stumbled at Middlesbrough, where they were 4-1 down with half an hour to play and they had Billy Cook sent off for a bad foul. Cook refused to leave the pitch and the referee abandoned the game. There was some controversy over whether the result would stand and in the end it did, but Cook's behaviour was so poor that he was eventually banned for a year. In the final analysis the Middlesbrough game was very costly, both for Oldham and Cook, who won little sympathy. Nothing was quite the same after Ayresome Park and when Oldham's directors decided to field Cook after the controversy, they received fierce criticism from the public and authorities.

Blackburn, trying to retain their title, lost four of their final six and the Latics imploded in April. The teams who had run into form were Everton, Burnley and Sheffield United. Burnley, in particular, proved to be a thorn in the side of the contenders, beating Everton at Goodison Park, drawing with Bradford and putting the first nail in Oldham's coffin.

Oldham were back on top with a fortnight to go, having beaten Sheffield United 3-0 at home, exacting some revenge for their FA Cup defeat to the Blades. Their final away game was at Villa Park, but they had to endure a frustrating afternoon as the home team held them to a goalless draw. Everton, on the same day, pulled off a very important 1-0 win at Manchester City and in doing so, went to the top of the table. They were ahead of Oldham on goal average but while Everton had one game remaining, Oldham had two to go – both at home. They were still favourites to come top, but they went into the final matches in hesitant form.

The first was against in-form Burnley. The visitors, a polished team who had risen up the league table, went into a two-goal lead against a nervous Oldham side. Walters pulled one back late in the day and the final minutes saw an onslaught from the Latics. It was to no avail, however, and the defeat proved catastrophic. The matter was no longer in Oldham's hands – they were level on points with Everton, but it meant that not even a win in their final game against Liverpool would give them the title as Everton had a far superior goal average. The Burnley defeat had all but destroyed Oldham's chances.

On the day of the famous 'Khaki Cup Final' between Chelsea and Sheffield United at Old Trafford, a dispirited Latics side lost 2-0 at a gloomy Boundary Park to Liverpool thanks to two goals from Fred Pagnam, a player who testified against his team-mates in the infamous 1915 football betting scandal. Charlie Roberts was at fault for the killer second goal in what was to be his last Football League game for the club.

Everton only had to turn up to confirm their success at Goodison Park against relegation-threatened Chelsea. They drew 2-2 and finished one point better off than Oldham. It had been a far from classic season with Everton's 46-point winning total the lowest since The Wednesday's 42 points in 1903. Only six points separated the top 11 clubs and Everton finished with just 18 points more than bottom-placed Tottenham.

Oldham, who had looked the most likely champions a few weeks earlier, had collapsed right at the end, perhaps due to a lack of experience, but some newspapers said there had been internal problems at the club which may have undermined their title bid. Certainly, most journalists felt that in the first half of the programme, Oldham were the best and most consistent team with some highly promising players such as 24-year-old Elliott Pilkington.

But the Cook affair had left a bit of a stain and more than one reporter said the Latics were still on something of a learning curve in league football. Another hack didn't mince his words, 'Few will deny Everton's absolute right to the honour. Even a week ago, Oldham Athletic looked to have the better chance, but they gradually tailed off and the finish – a defeat at home to Liverpool – is almost pathetic.'

The club continued to lose money in 1914/15 and their revenues dropped to £9,723 with £5,013 being paid out in wages. Their gate receipts for the season totalled £6,512, which amounted to the lowest since they joined the Football League. Most of professional football suffered similarly, some clubs faring much worse.

It was to be the last proper league season until 1919/20, after the war had concluded in 1918. The footballing authorities finally decreed that the Football League and FA Cup would cease until further notice for a variety of reasons. Many players had now enlisted, either independently or through footballers' units. Oldham's Jimmie Broad signed up just after the final league game. Others were involved in munitions work. This left many clubs depleted of playing resources. Furthermore, long railway journeys to away games were impossible, as well as overnight stays. The financial situation was also worsening, with attendances falling and public opinion turning ever more negative.

There was talk of football just being played as friendlies, but another scheme was discussed to operate a league that would include Oldham as well as Celtic, Rangers, Hearts, Hibernian and other northern clubs. In the end, Oldham were part of the Lancashire Section Principal Tournament, which included the clubs from Liverpool, Manchester and the surrounding areas. Oldham, who could call on the bulk of their 1914/15 side during the war leagues, finished fifth.

By the time 'normal' football resumed in 1919, the world was a different place. Six million men were mobilised in the United Kingdom and around 700,000 were killed. As well as Jimmie Broad, other players from the 1914/15 team who served in the army during the war included Arthur Cashmore, Ted Taylor, Bill Goodwin, Hugh Moffat and Joe Walters.

As for Oldham's fortunes, they struggled in the early postwar years, eventually suffering relegation in 1923. Their next top-flight season was in 1991/92. Nobody will ever know what might have happened if the 'Great War' hadn't got in the way of that 1915 team.

3

Cardiff City 1924:
Beaten by the law of averages

NOBODY REALLY understood goal average, especially in the days before the pocket calculator was invented in 1970. The mechanics of the system meant if an outcome was to be decided by goal average, the arithmetic couldn't easily be worked out on the back of a cigarette packet. Imagine, then, being denied footballing glory by the narrowest of margins, a slide-rule calculation that divided the number of goals scored by the number of goals conceded.

In 1923/24, Cardiff City were agonisingly close to winning their first league title. They were outdone by Huddersfield Town by 0.024 of a goal. If goal difference had been in play, Cardiff and Huddersfield would have finished on +27 but the Welshmen would have been champions by virtue of scoring one goal more than the Terriers. Cardiff are still awaiting that first championship and in an age of fabulously wealthy clubs, it would seem unlikely that the Bluebirds will ever be in such a strong position again.

Cardiff in the 1920s was enjoying its status as a city, an honour bestowed upon it in 1905 by King Edward VII. But life in the years between the two world wars was hard for its people, with unemployment and poverty levels very high.

Much of this was due to a decline in demand for Welsh coal exports. In 1924, unemployment among miners was around five per cent, but this more than doubled to 12.5 per cent the following year. At one stage, Cardiff's Tiger Bay was the world's most important coal port; and Cardiff's docks handled a greater tonnage than both London and Liverpool.

Cardiff itself had a population of just under 200,000 people in the 1920s and the football club could call on a sizeable percentage of them for support. They averaged 32,000 per game at Ninian Park in the 1921/22 season, a figure that has seldom been bettered in their history. Even though Cardiff was a rugby stronghold and the club was in the heart of rugby territory, the backing of the working-class folk of the city was passionate and intimidating for visitors.

The Bluebirds were not just representing a city, however; they also became one of the standard-bearers of Welsh football. Their ground was the principal home of the national team and their players were very influential in the red-shirted Welsh side.

Cardiff were founded in 1899 as Riverside AFC at the home of a lithographic artist, Bartley Wilson. The club changed its name to Cardiff City in 1908 and two years later joined the Southern League. In 1913 they were promoted to the top division after winning the second tier, losing just one game in the process. They were elected to the Football League in 1920 in a year in which the Third Division was formed with the expansion of the competition south of Birmingham, a move that decimated the Southern League.

Cardiff joined the Football League Second Division along with Leeds United, the Bluebirds receiving 23 votes to Grimsby Town's 20. The club ran a good campaign to win support, pointing to their ground, their support, their talented squad of players and their strong finances. In 1919/20, Cardiff's total gate receipts amounted to £28,000 which equated to £900 for every home game.

The *Athletic News* noted Cardiff's biggest selling point was the local populace that was 'mad for the best football'. They were, said the publication, the most convincing candidate for the league since Tottenham Hotspur. As a business, Cardiff produced a formidable claim to be a member of the Football League. Some commentators were less enthused, saying the club's election was a triumph of finance over sentiment. Football had become a commercial enterprise, a transition that had driven higher wages and heavier expenses.

Cardiff spent a lot of money, £20,000 on Ninian Park alone, ahead of their first season in the Football League. It was a memorable debut for the Bluebirds, who won their first game 5-2 against Stockport County and rarely looked back. Not only did they win promotion to the First Division at the first attempt but they also reached the semi-finals of the FA Cup, losing to fellow Second Division side Wolverhampton Wanderers after a replay. Cardiff became something of a 'media darling' with journalists claiming they were the team of 1920/21 and that the Football League's 'new baby' had become a thriving infant.

The momentum continued into 1921/22, but not before Cardiff had struggled in the early weeks of the campaign, losing their first six games. It looked as though they were out of their depth but their recovery was notable, eventually finishing fourth although they were nine points behind champions Liverpool, who they beat just before the end of the league programme.

The team that would eventually go so close to being champions was taking shape. Their first captain in the Football League, Charlie Brittain, retired before the 1922/23 season, leaving Scottish defender Jimmy Blair to take over the captaincy. Fred Keenor, who became a club legend, was named as vice-captain.

Continuity was an important factor in Cardiff's success. Their manager, Fred Stewart, ran the team for 22 years, taking the role on in 1911 and relinquishing it in 1933. 'We get players of decent ability and each man does his best, with unity of feeling and purpose. We never make a change in the team without consulting with the players. Their opinion is worth having,' he told one newspaper of the time.

In a very short time frame, Stewart and his players had come from the Southern League to the top division of the Football League. The 1922/23 season was tougher, despite the addition of young Irish goalkeeper Tom Farquharson from Abertillery. The tide turned after a six-game losing streak when Liverpool, the reigning champions and league leaders, were beaten 3-0 at Ninian Park in late October. But for the performance of goalkeeper Elisha Scott, Cardiff might have doubled the scoreline. At the time they were in the bottom two, but by the beginning of May 1923 Cardiff had reached ninth place.

There was only one major arrival in the close season of 1923, left-winger Denis Lawson, who joined from St Mirren. Most of the Cardiff team had been signed after the club gained admission to the Football League, although the first player to be bought for money was Jack Evans back in 1910. A loyal clubman who spent more than 16 years with Cardiff, Evans cost the grand sum of six shillings (30p), which also included his fare from Treorchy.

Evans came from Bala, a small town with a population below 2,000 and renowned for the manufacture of hosiery and gloves. The left-winger with a fierce shot was capable of being a dazzling performer, but earlier he sustained a bad shoulder injury that threatened to prematurely end his football career.

A year later, Billy Hardy was signed from Stockport County for £25, a fee that was paid by Stewart because Cardiff were in dire straits financially. When Stewart arrived at the club in 1911 they were losing money and living precariously on an overdraft, but under his stewardship, the Bluebirds were able to turn things around.

A massively popular player with Cardiff's fans, Hardy was born in Bedlington but played briefly for Heart of Midlothian. His move to Cardiff, where he was known as 'the idol of South Wales', seemed to prevent him from winning a cap for England, despite being highly rated across the football community.

Keenor, the man immortalised outside their new Cardiff City Stadium by a statue, joined the club in 1912, initially as an amateur but shortly afterwards as a professional, earning ten shillings a week (50p). 'It was always my ambition to play for the club,' insisted Keenor some years later.

Keenor was the original club hero, loyal, reliable, a leader and consistent. Additionally, he fought in the First World War after signing on for national service in 1915, the ninth player from the club to have responded to the great patriotic call. Keenor joined the 17th Middlesex (the Footballers' Battalion) just as he had established himself in the Cardiff side.

Keenor was at the Battle of the Somme and was wounded by shrapnel, so much so that doctors told him he had no future as a sportsman. He would go on to captain the club, replacing Jimmy Blair, and led Cardiff to their monumental 1927 FA Cup victory. He also captained Wales, for whom he appeared 32 times between 1920 and 1932.

In Cardiff's last season in the Southern League, they signed a young forward from local club Victoria Athletic, Len Davies. A frail-looking figure, Davies was from Splott, south of Cardiff. He took time to settle and was not a first choice until 1921. Cardiff had brought in an experienced head in Fred Pagnam, a much-travelled forward who cost £3,000. Pagnam, whose name was tainted by his involvement in the 1915 betting scandal when he was with Liverpool, helped Cardiff win promotion to the First Division in 1920/21, their inaugural Football League campaign, but had struggled to score goals at a higher level. He was sold to Watford for £1,000 and Davies grabbed the chance to secure a regular place in the first team. Davies went on to score prolifically for Cardiff and remains, to this day, their record goalscorer. He was also capped 23 times by Wales, scoring six goals.

Billy Grimshaw had also joined Cardiff in 1919. Born in Burnley and the son of a Blackburn Olympic footballer, Grimshaw fought in the First World War, reaching the rank of bombardier, and despite taking his time to enjoy success he was highly rated. His speed and skilful technique made him a popular player and although full international honours didn't come his way, he did represent the Football League. Grimshaw wanted to leave Cardiff and play for a club closer to Bradford where he could also play cricket in the summer months, but he was eventually sold to Sunderland for £5,000 halfway through the 1923/24 season.

Over the next few years, Cardiff assembled a team considered to be an expensive group of players, even though half of the squad had cost nothing. In 1920, three important players arrived: Jimmy Blair, Jimmy Gill and Herbie Evans. Blair was 32 when he arrived at Ninian Park, and his career had been hampered by a bad motorcycle accident when he was with The Wednesday. He had fallen out with Wednesday even though they had gone to great lengths to keep the Scottish international. Although approaching the veteran stage of his career, Blair was still considered a polished and brilliant defender and was worth every penny of the £4,000 Cardiff paid for his services.

Cardiff also paid a sizeable fee for another Wednesday player, Jimmy Gill. Wednesday were in financial trouble and needed the money and in Gill, Cardiff picked up a goalscorer and a player capable of skilful, intricate dribbling.

The other major signing in 1920 was Herbie Evans, who joined from local amateur side Cardiff Corinthians. He remained an amateur for much of his time with the club, but eventually turned professional and almost immediately broke his leg. He was out of the game for a couple of seasons before joining Tranmere, where he suffered a second break. Although seemingly an unlucky player, Evans was a popular fellow and won six caps for Wales.

When Joe Clennell joined Cardiff in 1921, it was because his club, Everton, thought he was finished. He was 32 years old and he had seen a lot of action, winning the Football League not just with Everton (1915), but also Blackburn Rovers (1912). Cardiff paid £1,500 for him and managed to get three good years out of him before he departed to Stoke City.

James Nelson was another arrival in 1921. He was a Scotsman who grew up in Northern Ireland and played for Crusaders before joining Cardiff. He won the FA Cup twice, with Cardiff in 1927 and then Newcastle United in 1932.

Cardiff were never seriously considered contenders in 1923/24. Liverpool had won the title in two consecutive seasons, both times by a six-point margin. Cardiff finished fourth in 1922 and dropped five places in 1923. Liverpool were favourites to make it a hat-trick of victories.

The opening day of the season produced its fair share of surprises, with Liverpool losing 2-0 at West Bromwich Albion. At the same time, Cardiff were beating Bolton Wanderers by the odd goal in five in front of 30,000 people at Ninian Park. Bolton were one of the more attractive visitors and earlier in 1923 had won the inaugural FA Cup Final at Wembley Stadium, beating West Ham United. Bolton would go on to become the cup kings of the 1920s, also winning the competition in 1926 and 1929.

Cardiff won again two days later, beating Sunderland 2-1 at home before travelling to Bolton to earn a good 2-2 draw.

The return game with Sunderland followed and Cardiff won 3-0 at Roker Park. Manager Fred Stewart was overjoyed, saying 'This was the greatest game I have ever witnessed and I have never seen our lads play such wonderful football.' Cardiff were brilliant and went to the top of the table, with Newcastle, Huddersfield and West Bromwich close behind, but it was still very early days.

Len Davies was in excellent form. In September 1923 his goals earned his team vital points against West Ham and Newcastle, the latter a 1-0 win at Ninian Park that saw Herbie Evans bravely play on with a bandaged head. Cardiff were two points clear with 13 points from eight games, having played two fewer than Bolton Wanderers and Aston Villa.

It wasn't until the 12th game of the season that Cardiff lost, the last team across the Football League's three divisions to be beaten. It was a costly defeat against bottom-of-the-table Preston North End at Deepdale. Preston won 3-1 and Huddersfield, who had beaten Birmingham, went top on goal average.

Cardiff bounced back well and beat West Brom twice, the second victory a stunning 4-2 success at The Hawthorns. Davies scored all four for the Bluebirds and they now led the table by one point with Huddersfield in second position.

Just before Christmas, Cardiff underlined their title credentials with two victories against reigning champions Liverpool. The first, at Anfield, almost announced a changing of the guard, with the Welshmen winning 2-0. 'North Wales and a sprinkling of the home faithful invaded Merseyside to pay tribute to the champion – which Cardiff may be, in the literal application of the term to the league tournament, in the fullness of time,' said one report.

Cardiff's teamwork was widely appreciated by the home crowd with Davies, 'the wisp of a boy who made up for his lack of physical power by his intelligence', causing Liverpool's defence untold problems. Cardiff scored a goal in each half and at the end, the 'effervescent winter air rang with national ardour'. The sound of 'Land of My Fathers' could be heard echoing across Anfield.

A week later, Cardiff won 2-0 again to go three points clear at the top of the table. The year ended, however, with their second setback, a 2-1 defeat at a packed Villa Park. The press called it a 'magnificent struggle' but Villa outplayed the leaders, who fielded an injury-hit team. Despite losing, Cardiff maintained top spot, two points better off than Bolton and four ahead of Huddersfield Town. Villa went to Wales and repeated the scoreline at Ninian Park against tired opponents who had to bring in a young winger, Billy Taylor, 'a ruddy boy from Redditch' who looked out of his depth. Still Cardiff led the field as Bolton failed to take advantage of the slip-up by drawing at home with Everton.

Cardiff embarked on their FA Cup run as they looked to put aside the loss of their unbeaten home record. They beat Gillingham (after a replay), Arsenal and Bristol City to reach the last eight. Cardiff's league form remained intact right up until the end of February, one notable victory being the 4-0 thrashing of Arsenal, who they would meet a few days afterwards in the FA Cup. That win, which saw Jimmy Gill net a hat-trick, put the Bluebirds four points clear of a bunch of tightly packed challengers, with just four points separating Bolton, Sunderland, Huddersfield, Aston Villa and Newcastle.

March was a torrid month for Cardiff, not just in the league but it also saw the end of their FA Cup hopes. It started with title rivals Huddersfield, managed by Herbert Chapman, beating them 2-0 at Leeds Road. Goalkeeper Tom Farquharson was absent owing to international duty with Ireland which meant Herbert Kneeshaw was selected. He could not be faulted for the two goals from former miner George Brown that won the game.

There were some critics who felt that Stewart's team was one that rode its luck and when the results started to turn against them, that they had it coming. To some extent there was a little bias against a Welsh side threatening to win the championship, but there could be no denying Cardiff had some exceptional players.

Little wonder the international selectors frequently came calling. In those days, home internationals would be played on the same day as league games so when, on 15 March, Notts County visited Ninian Park, Cardiff were missing Farquharson as well as Welshmen Fred Keenor, Len Davies and Herbie Evans, and the injured Joe Clennell. Cardiff simply didn't have the strength in depth to cope with such an obstacle and were beaten 2-0. It capped a miserable week as just a couple of days earlier, Manchester City had won 1-0 in Cardiff in the FA Cup quarter-final replay.

Cardiff, it would seem, could concentrate on the league title race, but the malaise that had descended upon them was difficult to shift. The Notts County defeat pushed Cardiff into third place, but they were arguably still the favourites as they had two games in hand on leaders Sunderland and were just three points worse off. Two more defeats, at Blackburn and Notts County, should have been more damaging than they were, but they were still only three points adrift even though they had dropped to fourth.

Clearly, Cardiff had lost their mojo and two goalless draws against Everton made the situation worse as they dropped to five points behind leaders Sunderland. At last, on 7 April 1924, they won their first league game in nine, a 2-1 victory against Tottenham. They didn't lose again until the season's end.

But the title race was now incredibly tight and Cardiff had allowed others to take centre stage, notably Huddersfield, who visited Ninian Park on 14 April. Accounts suggest it was the most momentous league match ever played at the ground and a thrilling exhibition of two of the best sides in Britain. Cardiff half-backs Harry Wake, Fred Keenor and Billy Hardy put on a dazzling display for the big crowd. Cardiff were the better team, but they could not find a way past their well-drilled opponents and the score remained goalless. Sadly, the game was marred by an incident near the end in which a miner, Gilbert Tarling, died in the Grangetown Stand. The draw sent Huddersfield to the top of the table, but only on goal average. There were three teams on 50 points – Huddersfield, Cardiff and Sunderland, a dynamic the media coined, 'a triangular tournament for the championship of the First Division'.

Sunderland eventually dropped out of contention, losing twice and drawing once in their last four games, but they still had enough energy to go top. Bolton, the outsiders, finished on 50 points, while Huddersfield still had matches to spare.

The Terriers, after beating Burnley 1-0 on 22 April, were top of the table but Cardiff were level on points. They were now most experts' tip for the title as they had three games to play versus Cardiff's two.

FA Cup Final day was on 26 April and Newcastle United beat Aston Villa at Wembley, but it was also a vital afternoon in the race for the championship. Huddersfield slipped up at Nottingham Forest, but Cardiff won 2-0 in their last home game in a one-sided victory against Birmingham City. Cardiff had a multitude of chances to improve their goal average, which given the lack of margin for error at the top of the table, became an important issue. Nevertheless, the two-goal win provided 'two golden points for the Welsh city'.

Huddersfield were just one point behind Cardiff but they had a game in hand, which they would play three days before the final Saturday of the campaign. Herbert Chapman's side showed signs of nerves and were beaten 3-1 at Villa Park.

The destination of the championship trophy was in Cardiff's hands. They had to travel to Birmingham on the last day, 3 May, while Huddersfield were at home to Nottingham Forest, who had been struggling at the foot of the table for most of the season. On the face of it, Cardiff were fancied to win the league – they had one point more than Huddersfield and a better goal average as they went into the final fixtures. Cardiff's goal average was 1.79 and Huddersfield's 1.72.

A 3-0 win for Huddersfield and a goalless draw for Cardiff would give the Yorkshiremen the title, and bizarrely that was exactly how it ended. Cardiff were not at their best at St Andrew's even though Birmingham were below full strength. In the second half, Birmingham's robust half-back Percy Barton handled on the goal line when an effort from Davies looked goalbound following a melee in the penalty area. A penalty was awarded and Davies failed to score even though he hit his spot kick hard, but it was straight at Birmingham goalkeeper Dan Tremelling. Meanwhile, over at Leeds Road, Huddersfield were romping to a 3-0 win against Forest, completing a dismal day for Cardiff.

At the final whistle Cardiff had been held 0-0, precisely the result they didn't need although they did not deserve to beat Birmingham in what was a grim tussle. Davies was distraught as the news confirmed that the Bluebirds had been denied by the slenderest of margins – 0.024 of a goal. The public and the media were quick to console Davies, who had been a huge influence in the rise of Cardiff.

The people of the city remained proud of their team and made sure that when they arrived back in Wales, they would receive a hearty welcome. It was 10.25pm when thousands of people gathered at Cardiff station – on the platforms, in the subways and outside – to cheer their heroes back home. The crowd called for Davies, who was 'pale and tired' after the journey back from Birmingham, still reliving his penalty miss. But the supporters, who stampeded towards the carriages as the train arrived, carried the crestfallen figure on their shoulders and the Welsh international was overcome with emotion. Fred Keenor, who thought he had evaded the crowd in quietly trying to merge with the fans, was also lifted high by the supporters.

It was a moving occasion and one reporter remarked that it was difficult to realise Cardiff were not the Football League champions. Regardless of failing at the final hurdle, this was a golden time for the Bluebirds. In 1924/25 they dropped to mid-table but they reached the FA Cup Final, losing 1-0 to Sheffield United. In 1925 they signed striker Hughie Ferguson from Motherwell for £5,000 and he repaid them in 1927 by scoring the winning goal in the cup final against Arsenal.

The 1923/24 season will, undoubtedly, remain Cardiff's most notable 'what if?'; the moment in time when a proud group of players almost became champions of England. At least they lifted the FA Cup three years on, but how remarkable would it have been for a Welsh team to become champions of England?

4

Argentina 1930: The second best team in the world

FOR MANY people, Argentina were always the bad guys, the Rolling Stones to Brazil's Beatles. A notable and stylish kit, a tactical approach that has often been a heady mix of European grit, determination and Latin American flair and notorious fellows such as Antonio Rattín and the late Diego Maradona. In modern times, Lionel Messi has won Argentina many friends, although even with his presence, major honours have largely eluded South America's most intriguing football nation.

With a population of 45 million, many of whom have ancestors in Italy and Spain, Argentina is arguably more European than any other country in South America. Unsurprisingly, the game of football was introduced to the nation by the British.

Argentina today is seen as a frequently unstable country that has a high level of poverty and somewhat volatile politics. In 1913, Argentina was richer than France or Germany and twice as wealthy as Spain. But over the past 100 years the country's prosperity has fluctuated and its place among the hierarchy of nations has dropped significantly. In the 1920s, Argentina enjoyed a spell of impressive economic growth that started to lose momentum in 1928. This period coincided with the first golden age of Argentinian football.

When they won the first of their two World Cups in 1978, various commentators, along with the masses in Buenos Aires and other cities, felt it was a long overdue honour. Argentine football, either side of the Second World War, had a reputation for style and sophistication, albeit with a somewhat tough underbelly. The over-physical approach crystallised in the 1960s, thanks to some brutal club sides that came up against European teams in the World Club Championship, such as Racing Club and Estudiantes, but this first became evident in England during the 1966 World Cup, notably when Alf Ramsey called their robust team 'animals'.

Long before that, Argentina and their neighbours from across the River Plate, Uruguay, were considered progressive football countries that produced outstanding, artistic individuals who played the game beautifully.

It was mostly heresay, though, for the rest of the world rarely caught a glimpse of teams from the opposite side of the globe. What started to fuel interest in South America was the Olympic Games football competition in 1924. This was the first Olympic tournament to include a team from South America in the form of Uruguay. Argentina, who declined to travel to Paris for the Games, couldn't quite believe it when Uruguay won the gold medal, beating Switzerland in the final.

Nobody knew much about Uruguay, either as a nation or a football team, but their success sparked off huge interest in South America and publishers struggled to keep pace with public demand for maps of the region. Moreover, the Uruguayan style, based on short passing and sudden changes in pace, enthralled the crowds at the Olympics.

Such was the superiority of Uruguay that there was some relief the other team from the banks of the River Plate,

Argentina, were not present. It was clear these sides had given the world a fresh dimension for the game; the so-called *Rioplatense* football.

Argentina and Uruguay, who probably spurred each other on, had dominated South America in the 1920s. Argentina had won the South American Championship four times since 1921; Uruguay had been champions on three occasions. In addition, Argentina had been runners-up four times in that period. Argentina didn't lose often, but when they did, it was usually to Uruguay.

The 1924 Olympics proved to be highly influential in the development of football in South America, resulting in invitations from Europe for clubs to tour the continent. The Argentine national team had intended to embark on a tour following Uruguay's victory, but Boca Juniors replaced them and visited Spain, Germany and France. In total, they played 19 games and lost just three. The Argentine football authorities, so pleased with the performances of Boca, gave them the title 'Champion of Honour' in recognition. The tour did a lot for Boca, transforming them from a Buenos Aires team to a national institution.

Similarly, Europeans visited Argentina, Brazil and Uruguay, notably Chelsea in 1929, who experienced a tour that was often troublesome.

The Uruguay triumph of 1924 also alerted European clubs about the talent available in South America. In particular, some played on the links between Argentina and Italy and enticed footballers with Italian ancestry to join them. These were known as the *oriandi* and the first of these was Julio Libonatti, a 25-year-old from Rosario who moved from Newell's Old Boys to Torino in 1926. He went on to win 18 caps for Italy to add to the 15 he had been awarded by Argentina between 1919 and 1922. It wasn't that difficult to lure players away as professionalism didn't really take root until 1931.

Argentina had salt rubbed in their wounds by Uruguay in the South American Championship in November 1924. The Olympic gold medallists finished on top in the four-team competition, drawing 0-0 with Uruguay in Parque Central. Argentina were desperate to prove they were better than Uruguay, admitting they were both respectful and resentful of their neighbours' success.

Between 1924 and 1930, Argentina and Uruguay continued to jockey for position in South America. In 1925, Argentina, fielding no fewer than eight Boca players, hosted the three-team finals of the South American Championship. Uruguay withdrew because of internal problems, so the final line-up included the hosts along with Paraguay and Brazil.

Uruguay regained the continental title in 1926, beating Argentina in the final group in Santiago, Chile, and eventually finishing top with a 100 per cent record from four games. A year later, Argentina got their revenge, scoring 15 goals in three games, including a 3-2 victory against their old rivals.

When both teams went to Amsterdam for the 1928 Olympics, they were arguably at their peak and a little of the mystery surrounding countries from South America had been removed thanks to Uruguay's previous success. There was no South American Championship that year owing to the Olympics, but it was widely believed this was the strongest football competition ever staged, even though there was no representation from the United Kingdom as its nations had withdrawn early in 1928.

Argentina had problems getting to Europe and the necessary funding wasn't in place until just before the Games began. Nevertheless, the Dutch public and the Olympic community were keen to see the flamboyant Argentinians in action. Just before the football tournament kicked off, FIFA, aware that the time was approaching for a professional competition, largely due to the growing suspicion that some countries were paying players appearing in the amateur-only Olympic competition, announced that a football world championship would be launched in 1930.

Argentina kicked off their bid for Olympic gold on 29 May in the Olympic Stadium before barely 3,000 people. They beat the United States, the leading nation in terms of medals won at every Olympic Games since 1912, 11-2 with Boca Juniors' 24-year-old striker Domingo Tarasconi scoring four times.

Tarasconi, who was the most coveted forward in Argentine football in the early 1920s, ended up as the Olympic tournament's top marksman in Amsterdam with 11 goals.

Argentina were goal-happy in the competition, following up their win against the US with a 6-3 victory against Belgium. Tarasconi netted four times. Meanwhile, Uruguay had disposed of the Netherlands and Germany, still displaying the qualities of Olympic champions.

There was an underlying feeling Argentina had a far easier run than Uruguay. In the semi-finals, they met Egypt and won 6-0 (Tarasconi with three) while Uruguay faced Italy, who included some players who would eventually win the World Cup. If the Uruguayans were the top team from South America then Italy could lay claim to being the best from Europe. Uruguay won 3-2 thanks to a scintillating first half and so the final would match two countries who were close neighbours and big rivals. It was another feather in the cap for the *Rioplatense* game.

Argentina saw the final as an opportunity to reassert their authority and prove they were, after all, superior to Uruguay. Such was the attraction of a final between the two teams considered to be the best in the world that 250,000 applications for 40,000 tickets were received. As it turned out, 28,000 people watched the game in the Olympic Stadium on 10 June. The teams were well-matched and the final ended in a 1-1 draw. A replay was held three days later and Uruguay ran out 2-1 winners – still Argentina could not silence their noisy neighbours.

The Olympics effectively became a shop window for *Rioplatense* football and Argentinian players became targets of clubs in Europe, particularly Italy. South American players were appreciated for their sublime skill and artistry, which contrasted with the more functional European style. Exports had started in the mid-1920s with Julio Libonatti. After the Olympics, Raimundo Orsi, a cultured left-winger, moved from Independiente to Juventus and won five Serie A titles with the Turin-based club as well as the World Cup with Italy in 1934.

In 1929, Uruguay, as arguably the best team in the world and because the country was less affected by the global financial crisis that was unfolding, was appointed to host the inaugural FIFA World Cup, despite interest from Italy, the Netherlands, Spain and Sweden. Also in 1929, Argentina hosted the South American Championship and beat Uruguay 2-0 to secure the title in the Estadio Gasómetro, home of San Lorenzo. By now, the *Albiceleste* were being led by a two-man team comprising Francisco Olazar and his younger technical director Juan José Tramutola.

Between that success in November 1929 and the 1930 World Cup in July, Argentina played just one more game, a 1-1 draw with Uruguay in the Newton Cup in Buenos Aires.

Uruguay, some felt, were past their best after their Olympic double and Argentina's gifted team fancied their chances of winning the Jules Rimet Trophy. The rivalry between the two nations wasn't just on the field, either; the fans also gave their opponents a hard time, constantly jeering each other.

Argentina started their World Cup campaign against France, one of only four teams from Europe to participate. The French, who had beaten Mexico 4-1 just two days earlier, were a tough nut to crack and it was not until the 81st minute that Luis Monti scored the winner. Monti, who was capable of a strong-arm approach, took out one of the key French players, Lucien Laurent, with a bad tackle and also repeatedly intimidated the impressive Marcel Pinel throughout the game. Monti, who would later move to Italy with Juventus, became an Italian international after winning 16 caps for Argentina and played in the infamous 'Battle of Highbury' against England, breaking his foot in a combative 90 minutes. It was the tough midfielder who scored the winner against France nine minutes from time.

Their second group game was against Mexico. Guillermo Stábile, a 25-year-old Huracán striker, was handed his international debut as the first choice, Boca's Roberto Cherro, suffered an anxiety attack after fainting in the game with France. Stábile, a short and pugnacious attacker, responded to the challenge with gusto, scoring a hat-trick and going on to become the World Cup's first leading scorer with eight goals. Yet the four caps he won in Uruguay were the only international appearances of his career. Argentina won 6-3 against Mexico and they completed their first phase programme by beating Chile 3-1 in the newly built Estadio Centenario in Montevideo.

While it was shaping up well for Argentina, hosts Uruguay were also heading towards the closing stages. They beat Peru and Romania, scoring five times while keeping their own goal intact. Although crowds flocked to the games, Uruguay seemed to lack some of the swagger of the team that had won the Olympics with such panache. In the semi-finals, both Argentina and Uruguay won 6-1, against the United States and Yugoslavia respectively.

So it was to be a local derby for the final. Argentina were marginal favourites, but Uruguay had home status so there could scarcely have been a more evenly matched final, nor one where the passions became so irrationally heated. Such was the bad feeling created by the build-up and aftermath of the final, but also due to several violent incidents during the competition, that some media commentators were very critical of the way football had been hijacked by nationalism.

In Buenos Aires, World Cup fever was raging as thousands of Argentinians clamoured for tickets and a passage to Montevideo, a journey of around 200km. The port of Buenos Aires had rarely been as frantic as rich and poor, young and old attempted to find a way across the estuary. The fog on the river was dense and amid the mayhem, an inbound flight from the US to Montevideo, presumably full of people heading for the final, crashed into the sea en route. The media in Argentina and Uruguay also did their best to fuel hatred, stirring up the only real South American football rivalry in existence at the time.

Although the Argentina team was staying in Santa Lucía, a city some 60km north-west of the centre of Montevideo, the Uruguayan supporters hunted them down and surrounded their hotel. There was no peace for the team, who were also visited by the famous French-Argentine singer and actor, Carlos Gardel, who was renowned for his association with the tango. He introduced a new tango to his repertoire as a tribute to Argentina's footballers.

More angst was to follow, though, with some Argentine players receiving death threats, notably Luis Monti, who was told that if his team won then his mother would be killed. Monti initially refused to play and Alberto Chividini was lined up to replace him, but at the 11th hour a sheepish and worried Monti changed his mind. It was a mistake, for Monti was largely ineffective and some reporters felt he should not have been included.

Over in Buenos Aires, Argentine fans chanted 'death to Uruguay' and 'Argentina si, Uruguay no!' on the quayside of the port. Unsurprisingly, the city virtually came to a standstill as the final approached, with shops and businesses closing and even intense production-line industries such as General Motors stopped their factories while the sensitive issue of the World Cup was decided. All of the pressure, the neurosis and displays of allegiance were completely missed in Europe, where the World Cup was receiving scant coverage.

The morning of the big game, billed as the biggest neighbourhood final in football (*final de barrio*) was tense beyond belief. The referee, John Langenus, was so concerned about his personal safety that he demanded protection. The official attendance at the Estadio Centenario was 68,346 but estimates of the true size of the crowd ranged from 70,000 to 90,000. Furthermore, there were around 10,000–15,000 people outside the stadium, eager to interpret the noises coming from inside the gleaming white arena.

It was a final that was too close to call, although the general consensus was that Argentina had the more sophisticated team. If they had the best forward in Stábile, Uruguay had probably the outstanding defender of the age in José Nasazzi, one of the first sweepers in football. He could be an uncompromising opponent and was known as *El Gran Mariscal*, the Great Marshal, due to his organisational skills as Uruguay's skipper. Throughout the final, Nasazzi teased and tussled with the Argentina players, prompting Jules Rimet himself to admit after the game that it had been a tough and uncompromising 90 minutes.

It was played before a hostile, partisan crowd that unnerved the Argentinian team, who had also received incredible abuse before the game. 'We were afraid they would kill us,' admitted Argentina's Francisco 'Pancho' Varallo. Intimidation wasn't restricted to Argentina, though, for there was an attempt to bribe Uruguay's Héctor Castro to throw the game, with the possibility of death if he did not comply.

Uruguay opened the scoring on 12 minutes, Pablo Dorado receiving the ball from Castro and shooting past Juan Botasso. Argentina were level eight minutes later through winger Carlos

Peucelle. Stábile scored his eighth goal of the competition in the 37th minute to give Argentina a half-time lead. Uruguay's second-half display turned the game on its head. 'Uruguay beat us because they were more alive and courageous,' said Varallo some years later. 'We should have won.'

Uruguay levelled in the 57th minute through Pedro Cea and nine minutes later, Santos Iriarte put the hosts ahead once more. The cup was secured with a fourth goal right at the end from Castro. Argentina's players couldn't bear to watch as Uruguay celebrated, kissing their light blue shirts. In Uruguay, a national holiday was declared as the country went wild with excitement.

Across the water in Argentina, the mood was very different, almost toxic. The Uruguayan consulate was attacked and gunfire and shootings prevailed across Buenos Aires. The local press were very harsh on their team, accusing them of 'lacking guts and courage'. Although Argentina's players were technically superior to their opponents and they had the potential to produce elegant and imaginative football, it was widely acknowledged they had lacked tactical nous. Varallo added, 'Uruguay beat us because they were sly.'

It was, perhaps, the end of the road for Argentina's team of the 1920s and eight of the players who appeared in the World Cup Final never put on the national shirt again. Frustratingly, Uruguay had beaten them yet again but they too would go through a transition.

Argentine football was on the brink of big changes, however, and within a few months, professionalism arrived. A dissident professional league, Liga Argentina de Football, started, and players started to demand freedom of contract. As money became the driving force in the domestic game, unsurprisingly, big-city clubs started to dominate.

When the next World Cup came around in 1934, a weakened Argentina went out of the competition rather cheaply. Italy won the next two World Cups and then war interrupted. When football resumed on the global stage in 1950, the competition was held in South America once more, but it was Uruguay who were triumphant again. Argentina's time would come much later.

5

Austria 1934: The end of *Das Wunderteam*

IN A cemetery on the outskirts of Vienna, the *Zentral Friedhof*, is the grave of Matthias Sindelar, one of Austria's greatest footballers. The site is not far from the resting places of some of the greatest musical composers of all time – Sindelar is indeed in good company, and rightfully so, for this legendary figure was one of the most remarkable players of his era and a superstar of the interwar years in Europe.

Sindelar was born in 1903 in Kozlov in Moravia, but moved to Vienna when he was just two years old. He was a rogueish youth and there were claims that his balletic style of play owed its roots to his antics as a youngster, running through the streets of Vienna with people in pursuit of him. An angular figure who seemed to glide in and out of challenges, Sindelar was nicknamed *Der Papierene*, the man of paper.

He became the figurehead of Austria's *Wunderteam*, a collection of supremely talented and cultured footballers who captured the imagination of the continent of Europe and, if mass media had been invented, would have also charmed the rest of the world. Sadly, *Das Wunderteam* peaked a little early for the World Cup cycle and were denied the chance to have their brilliance anointed. Having been the early 1930s' most captivating team, by the time the 1934 competition came around their silky football had been overtaken by the power of Italy. Within five years the mastermind of the team, Hugo Meisl, and his protégé Sindelar were both dead and the dream of Austrian football supremacy was over.

Austria have rarely looked as good since those halcyon days, but Meisl and his team have never been forgotten; they were so influential that traces of their innovative style can be found in the Hungarians of 1953, the Dutch of 1974 and even Barcelona's team of 2011. For Johan Cruyff and Rinus Michels you could quite easily read Sindelar and Meisl or Messi and Guardiola. It wasn't always that way, for Sindelar had to convince Meisl he was the right man and that his own style was aligned to Meisl's thinking about how the game should be played. Meisl relented in 1931, restoring Sindelar to the national team after public pressure to select the popular playmaker. Nevertheless, there was a chemistry between the two men and Sindelar became the highest-paid footballer in continental Europe.

The fluid, organic style, where the player with the ball is supported by his team-mates and gaps are filled by whoever is closest at hand, was a vision of the future. This style allowed Austria's fleet-footed team to move from defence to attack in a seamless manner and vice versa. It was not terribly dissimilar to the short-passing game adopted by Scotland at the time, but it introduced wide-running half-backs and an attacking centre-half, as well as a slightly deep-lying centre-forward. It was a Brit, Jimmy Hogan, who helped shape Meisl's footballing philosophy. Hogan's story is interesting, for he became something of a pariah in Britain after spending the First World War in Europe. But he became a pivotal figure in the growth of the game in *Mitteleuropa* despite being little-known in his home country. Meisl saw Hogan as an acolyte and helped him out of prison during the war, allowing him to seek refuge in Budapest.

When Austria visited England in 1932, Hogan trained the team and barked his instructions in English, to the amazement of the media who had not realised who he was. Meisl was always quick to praise the contribution of Hogan, claiming he had taught so many countries about the science of the game.

Austrian football developed from the late 19th century, initially in the city of Graz. Several clubs sprung up in this period: Wiener SC were formed in 1883, then First Vienna and the Vienna Cricket and Football Club – which still resides in the shadow of the Prater Stadium – were founded in 1894, and Rapid followed five years later. In 1904, the Vienna Football Association was formed. By the 1930s the Austrian capital had 35 professional clubs, including Rapid, the favourite of working-class folk and the epitome of proletarian toughness, and FK Austria Wien, a club that stood for the city, patronised by Jewish liberals.

It is easy to stumble across culture and academia in a city like Vienna and it's a rather nice idea that bohemian scholars and the artistic element played their part in developing the central European approach to football in the interwar years. In places like Café Central on the Herrengasse, pencil-bearded professors debated the W-M formation or the exploits of *Das Wunderteam* – perhaps alongside representatives from the Vienna Circle of Logical Positivists. Writers often called Vienna a 'centre of fermentation', driven by the cultural and intellectual elite. Ideas, ideologies, social movements, progressive medicine, music and literature filled the air of Vienna's cafes. There's no football connection to be found in Café Central, or any other of the Viennese coffee houses anymore – Café Holub and Café Parisfal were also both popular football haunts in days gone by. Visitors today, as they scoop the frothy milk off the finest Arabica, have little idea they may be sitting where sporting history had been shaped.

The Jewish community was also instrumental in the development of football in central Europe. Jews, who often found they were up against severe prejudice in interwar Austria, often combatted isolation by creating their own groups and societies, including football clubs. Jewish football people, such as Hugo and Willy Meisl, would sit in coffee houses and discuss football and develop a new way of playing, which became known as the Danubian style.

Vienna was also a driver of the first major pan-European competition. The original idea of a European football tournament dates back to the late 19th century. It was undoubtedly a product of the Austro-Hungarian empire. Needless to say, this competition, which ran from 1897 to 1911, was dominated by teams from Vienna, Budapest and Prague. After the First World War, the concept of a European football competition gathered momentum. By this time, professionalism had swept across the region and in Vienna in 1927, the Mitropa Cup was born.

Hugo Meisl, at the time the head of the Austrian Football Association, was the biggest advocate of *La Coupe de l'Europe Centrale*. His experiences during the First World War in Serbia helped form a belief that sport, and football in particular, could help develop unity between nations.

The organisers wanted the strongest possible field, mostly drawn from the capital cities, which may actually have been purely down to commercial reasons. In Austria, Admira Vienna had won the league and they, along with Rapid Vienna, were invited to take part. The first final, however, was between Sparta Prague and Rapid Vienna. It was the sort of decider that Meisl and his colleagues must have yearned for, but the cup went to Czechoslovakia. The Mitropa Cup went from strength to strength, but its halcyon days were in the pre-Second World War period. It provided a blueprint for what was to follow in the 1950s. After the World Cup, the Mitropa Cup was arguably the most significant competition in the interwar period and the list of finalists reads like a who's who of central European football in the 1920s and 1930s.

Meisl was instrumental in the creation of the Central European International Cup, also known as the Dr Gerö Cup. This competition, for national teams, was played over two or more years. The first series, played between 1927 and 1930, saw Italy come top and Austria joint second with Czechoslovakia. But the second series, held from 1931 to 1932, ended with Austria winning the trophy, largely thanks to a 2-1 victory against Italy in March 1932, a game in which Sindelar scored twice and the legendary Guiseppe Meazza responded for Italy, who included five players who would win the World Cup in 1934.

At the time, Meisl's team was in tremendous form and had become known as *Das Wunderteam*, a tag that emerged after Meisl told reporters in a Viennese cafe, 'Da habt's euer Schmiranski-Team,' which loosely translated meant the Austrians had a team that lubricated the mind. It was also a team that was familiar with the concept of international competition, at both national and club level.

The actual *Wunderteam* started life in May 1931 when they impressively beat Scotland 5-0 in Vienna and could have reached double figures were it not for goalkeeper John Jackson, who kept the Austrian forwards at bay. This game started a spectacular sequence of results, which included satisfying 6-0 and 5-0 wins against Germany, an 8-1 victory in Switzerland and a 2-2 draw with arch-rivals Hungary.

In December 1932 the British public caught a glimpse of a team in its prime, but the nation still considered that the home of football produced the finest players on the planet. This feeling was enhanced by a 7-1 victory against Spain at Arsenal's Highbury in December 1931, although the London media were not impressed with the Spanish players' behaviour or demeanour. This was still an insular time and foreigners were treated with some suspicion. That victory restored faith in England after they had been beaten 5-2 in Paris by the French team that appeared in the inaugural World Cup in 1930.

Meisl was an admirer of the English game, but he felt that it had become too mechanised due to the emphasis on league football. He felt England had a big advantage in that they had so many players to choose from, but warned that its insularity could become a handicap. 'The more contact England has with the outside world, the better for her game,' he said in an interview in Vienna. 'Our game is the study of many systems, for we are always playing other continental opponents.'

Meisl was outspoken with his friend, Herbert Chapman. He suggested that the defence-oriented approach of the Arsenal team of the 1930s didn't get the best out of supremely talented players like Alex James. Chapman responded, 'Look, Hugo, it works. It brings results. We English are so slow it will do for years. I am waiting until everyone else copies it and then I shall come up with something new.' It was Meisl who had come up with something fresh, rather than the English.

Austria included Rudi Hiden in their team, a talented goalkeeper who had been courted by Arsenal in 1930. The ministry of labour wouldn't allow Hiden to move to London after the Football Association and Players' Union protested and when he arrived at Dover with his Austrian team-mates in December 1932, he had to confirm he would be travelling home with the rest of the players and not seeking to stay in England. Hiden was only 21 when Arsenal pursued him and were willing to pay £2,500 for his services, but he lost his place in the Austrian squad in 1933 when he moved to France to play for Racing Club Paris. As the team proceeded to London's Victoria station, crowds of eager football fans were there to meet 16 fresh-faced and sensibly clothed young men in felt hats, cheering them as they left the train. They were described as Europe's champion nation, a title that they hadn't really earned, but it did, at least, show that their reputation went before them. Jimmy Hogan, their coach, told the press, 'Whatever happens, you will find our boys play real football.'

Meisl was also a figure of fascination with the British public. In 1933, the Scottish press said he was 'C.B. Cochran [a theatrical impresario], Mussolini and Herbert Chapman rolled into one'. He always wore spats and a long grey coat and pulled his bowler hat down to just above his eyes. His voice was 'stentorian' and gave the impression he was really a school master. 'One sound from him and the players don't do what they like,' was one verdict.

It was very clear Austria's players had a different approach and their style of play was far more imaginative. They seemed faster, more elegant and certainly more skilful with the ball. Their passing movements represented a more thoughtful way to play the game and a stark contrast to the slog of league football. When England hosted the Austrians at Stamford Bridge, they somehow managed to beat Meisl's team 4-3, but the press were convinced England were very fortunate to have won. The London public was, generally, thrilled by the display of the foreigners who were unlucky to have lost. Indeed, most of the plaudits went to the Austrians, who were 'a really great side', and the belief was that England may have won but they rarely played like an international team. Back in Vienna, the city's factories and offices came to a standstill as the game was broadcast on radio. When England scored their four goals, gasps of horror could be heard all over the capital. Leading up to the team's trip to London, the possibility of defeat was not even contemplated.

Meanwhile, the 42,000 people at Stamford Bridge were kept on the edge of their seats and the result was in doubt right to the end. England led by two goals at half-time but

Karl Zischek pulled one back just after the break. England restored a two-goal advantage but then Sindelar ran through to make it 3-2. Sammy Crooks added another for the English but Zischek reduced the arrears once more. At the final whistle, they were relieved to have beaten the team everyone was calling the unofficial world champions, and furthermore, it allowed England to go on believing they were still the masters, given they had no inclination to play in a World Cup.

There were two years until the next World Cup and the geo-political atmosphere in central Europe was fragile. In 1933, parliamentary democracy in Austria was under pressure and was gradually being eroded. Over in Germany, Adolf Hitler became chancellor and, as an Austrian, he eyed the possibility of annexing the country of his birth. Austria's own chancellor, Engelbert Dollfuß, made friends with Benito Mussolini and *Il Duce* assured him that if Austria was ever under threat, he would help defend the nation.

Dollfuß took advantage of a loophole in parliamentary voting to develop a one-party state and champion *Austrofascism*. Early in 1934, Austria had a four-day uprising which some called a civil war. It was fascism against socialism and the outcome meant that football was affected in that the right-wing state tried to influence who was selected for the national team. It was the beginning of the end for the *Wunderteam* because the regime that created the team that expressed the artistic and cultural heart of Austria and Vienna, almost as much as the works of Klimt, Mahler and Schnitzler, was losing its sponsor – Red Vienna. This was a Vienna that was dominated by social democrats and left-wing radicals, a time that laid the foundations for the social welfare state, a system copied throughout Europe. The problem was that Red Vienna now no longer existed as Austria lurched towards their menacing neighbours, so any footballer who was openly opposed to the Dollfuß administration could be vulnerable.

Sindelar wasn't the only character loved by coffee house society. Walter Nausch, the captain of the team, was something of an intellectual and spoke excellent English. He was a bank clerk until his employer, Creditanstalt, crashed during the financial crisis of the period. Nausch, a very popular figure, often spoke out against the regime because he felt protected. However, Nausch was married to a Jew and was later instructed to leave his wife after Austria was occupied by Germany. He refused and fled to Switzerland where he forged a career as a coach. In 1934, Nausch was badly injured playing against Bulgaria and consequently missed the World Cup.

Anton Schall was another likeable fellow, largely due to his matinee idol looks and his perpetual smile. Schall, between 1925 and 1941, scored 231 goals in 285 games for Admira Vienna. Sadly, Schall died aged only 40 due to a rare heart condition. This wasn't evident during his career, when his pace and ability marked him as one of Austria's greatest ever players.

Wiener AC's Karl Sesta, a defender who represented both Austria and Germany, was not only renowned for his robust play and man-marking skills, but also his singing. Many said he would have made a career as an opera singer had he not chosen football. An eclectic character, he started out as a wrestler and was also a trained blacksmith.

Karl 'Pipsi' Zischek spent 20 years with FC Admira and won over 40 caps for Austria. His speed and ball control astounded football fans across Europe. He earned the nickname 'Ghost', for his ability to arrive in the penalty area totally unopposed.

Nausch's absence would be a blow to Austria, but they were still among the favourites for the 1934 World Cup in Italy, even though some experts felt the team that had charmed Europe was possibly past its peak. Of the team that ran England close in 1932, only five members were in Meisl's squad for Italy. Rudi Hiden, Karl Rainer, Walter Nausch, Karl Gall, Fritz

Gschweidl and Leopold Vogt were not included. In Nausch's absence, Josef Smistik captained the team. He was a defensive midfielder who worked as a motor mechanic before become a professional. Smistik was known for his stamina and ability to hit long balls from one end of the pitch to the other.

Sindelar, of course, was the star of the show and attracted a lot of attention. He was 31 years of age at the time but was still coveted by managers and coaches. Arsenal, for example, wanted to sign Sindelar after the 1932 England game and had kept tabs on him for over two years.

David Goldblatt, in his magnificent tome *The Ball is Round*, suggested the *Wunderteam* was 'tired and troubled' when arriving in Italy. The politics of Austria and the constant attention on the team and its methods was starting to wear them down. Certainly, the press and experts felt Italy, with home advantage and several players who had moved from Argentina and repatriated, would be the most fancied team.

Austria struggled to reproduce their best form in the World Cup, as evidenced when they only marginally won through against France in the first round. The French took the lead and although Sindelar equalised, the game went to extra time. Austria, thanks to goals from Schall and the young Josef Bican, took control but a very late strike from the French made it a nervous finale.

The quarter-final paired Austria with Hapsburg neighbours Hungary. Meisl brought in Johan Horvath, the 31-year-old FC Wien inside-left, and he gave the *Wunderteam* the lead early on. Zischek added a second in the second half and Hungary scored on the hour to put some pressure on Austria. The game was a catalogue of fouls and irritations, perhaps unsurprisingly as the two nations were fierce rivals.

Austria faced Italy in the semi-final in the San Siro stadium in Milan. Many felt this should have been the natural final in 1934, but most of the pressure was on Italy. On the eve of the game, Mussolini had dinner with the match officials so there was a hint of corruption in the air. Stories abound that the Swedish referee, Ivan Eklind, was instructed to let Italy win the tie. At the very least, the match officials were intimidated.

The swampy pitch at the San Siro certainly hampered Austria and their free-flowing style. Zischek and Sindelar found the heavy conditions difficult and the Italians, notably Luis Monti, used over-zealous methods to keep the talented Austrians quiet. Italy won 1-0 with a first-half goal from the Argentinian-born Enrique Guaita. Zischek almost equalised in the final seconds, but Austria left the field knowing an era had come to an end.

Indeed it had, for Austria lost something in the aftermath of the World Cup. Meisl had also lost some impetus. In 1935, after receiving considerable criticism for Austria's failure in Italy, Meisl tried to resign, claiming, 'I am tired and overworked and I feel I must be relieved of some of my numerous offices.' He wanted to stand down from having responsibility for the national team, although he would retain his job as secretary-general of the Austrian Football Association. He carried on until his sudden death in 1937, his last game in charge being a 2-1 win against France in the Parc des Princes, Paris.

Austria was annexed to Germany and that was the end of the nation's football team. Sindelar himself met a controversial end after making enemies of the wrong people. In a so-called 'Anschluss match' in April 1938, Sindelar scored a goal for Austria against Germany and appeared to taunt Nazi officials. The regime saw Sindelar as a Jewish sympathiser and he became a marked man with the Gestapo keeping a file on him. In January 1939, Sindelar and his girlfriend, Camilla Castagnola, were found dead in his apartment in Favoriten. There has always been an air of mystery about his death, but the official verdict was that a milk pan had fallen from a gas stove and the flame had been extinguished. The apartment filled with carbon monoxide and poisoned the couple. On the other hand, some felt he had simply been murdered.

Sindelar, Meisl and the *Wunderteam* have lived on, the subject of frequent speculation about what they might have achieved. They had their moment in the sun, but it came when only a World Cup could have given them the credibility they deserved. Austria has rarely touched the heights of that wonderfully skilful team playing the 'Danubian Whirl' and they have seldom seen a player as richly talented as Sindelar. Rightfully, they are appropriately remembered in the pantheon of the game.

6

Brazil 1950: The men
of *Maracanazo*

BRAZIL HAS hosted two World Cups and both have ended in disaster, creating moments in time that became days, months and years of national mourning. The most recent, the 2014 semi-final loss at the hands of Germany, a calamitous 7-1 humbling, should have made amends for the first occasion, the 1950 defeat in the deciding game against Uruguay, but it merely added to the nation's list of black days.

One could be forgiven for thinking that, in the modern age of mass media and unnecessary hubris, a defeat in 2014 would be treated like the apocalypse, but the fateful 1950 final has never been erased from the Brazilian psyche. Seventy years later, the pain of losing a World Cup the country had considered to be theirs for the taking refuses to subside. One writer, the playwright Nelson Rodrigues, called the defeat by Uruguay and the impact on the population 'our Hiroshima'. Certainly, this game, on 16 July 1950, is a worthy entrant into Rodrigues's own 'theatre of the unpleasant'.

As the host nation, Brazil would always be considered among the favourites; the advantage of playing on their own soil and in their own climate was so great that most experts believed they would comfortably win the competition. The opportunities from staging the competition were manifold: firstly, the country was trying to portray itself as a modernist, progressive state that embraced the notion of internationalising Brazil. Secondly, Brazil had become fanatical about football and given the Second World War had not left too many scars on South America, FIFA decided to play the first tournament since 1938 many miles away from war-torn Europe. The Brazilians were only too aware that in two of the three competitions played since its inauguration the hosts – Uruguay and Italy – had lifted the Jules Rimet Trophy.

But it was more than mere football, although the value of the game as an integrating force was very much on FIFA's mind as the world started to repair broken bridges and relationships. Put simply, Brazil was desperate to host the World Cup and had been since the late 1930s. Initially, they had their eyes on 1938 and then the never-to-be 1942 competition, but the war put paid to any hope of that happening. Finally, in 1947, FIFA awarded the 1950 World Cup to Brazil.

At the time, Brazil was a country of 50 million people, many living far below the poverty line. Furthermore, life expectancy for a male was some 25 years shorter than in the United States. In the big cities, such as Rio de Janeiro and São Paulo, the poorest citizens gravitated towards the notorious favelas, large makeshift hillside communities characterised by crime and deprivation. These favelas grew during the 1950s through to the 1970s, but they also produced a lot of talented footballers. It was an escape route from the slums.

The World Cup was also seen as the chance to endorse the Brazilian democracy, which had been reintroduced in 1946 after around a decade of dictatorship. Eurico Gaspar Dutra was elected president at the end of January. All ties with the Soviet Union were severed and Brazil started to move closer to the United States. Exchange controls were implemented, exports discouraged and there was an aggressive drive to expand manufacturing. The country grew quite healthily; its GDP averaged 7.6 per cent per year during the Dutra era, with industry averaging nine per cent and agriculture 4.5 per cent. In the postwar world, sport was seen as a unifying force and the World Cup also had a big diplomatic task to fulfil.

When preparations began, it was clear the Brazilian energy and transport infrastructure was found wanting. In addition, 1950 was also a chance to bring urbanisation to Brazil and thus started a population shift. In 1950, 64 per cent of the country lived in the countryside.

Above all, the government wanted to build a football ground in Rio de Janeiro that would send a strong message to the rest of the world: the most modern, largest and most impressive stadium on the planet, one that would be a clear statement of intent. It would be called the Maracanã.

Just as the 2014 World Cup would have its detractors – socially minded folk who felt the money should be spent on hospitals and schools – the new stadium also came in for criticism, but the city council voted in favour of constructing 'a gift from this generation to the next'. The precise location of this stadium was another point of contention. The biggest antagonist was politician Carlos Lacerda, an opponent of the mayor of Rio, who wanted it to be built in the western district, Jacarepagúa, but radio broadcaster Ary Barroso was vocal in his support of a city centre site. The project, generally, was backed by the media, with the journalist Mário Filho of *Jornal dos Sports* a huge advocate.

Filho was the brother of Nelson Rodrigues and a hugely influential figure in the development of Brazilian football. It was Filho who coined the term 'Fla-Flu' to describe the Rio derby between Fluminense and Flamengo, and he was also instrumental in pushing the cause of black players, notably in his book, *O Negro no Futebol Brasileiro*. The Maracanã was eventually named after the man who was called the 'creator of crowds' by his playwright brother. This nickname was not given to him because of his support of the Maracanã – it was also a reflection of Filho's role in helping transform Brazilian football crowds into a glorified carnival. He also knew the value of good publicity and did his best to hype up games. As Alex Bellos said in his forensic study of Brazilian football, Filho blurred the lines between journalist, novelist and businessman.

The Maracanã wasn't the only new ground built for the World Cup; the Estádio Independência in Belo Horizonte, where England came unstuck against the United States, was also opened at the competition. Others, in Curitiba and Recife, were still relatively recent builds.

Constructing this grand site with a capacity of around 183,000 was such a huge task that seven architects were involved in the design. At the time there was nothing to match it; the brutalist design was very much the embodiment of modernity.

Brazil hadn't played any European opposition since the 1938 World Cup, the third/fourth-place play-off when they beat Sweden. They were denied a place in the final by eventual champions Italy. Since 1938 they had only played South Americans. In 1949, they hosted the South American Championship, a competition they had not won since 1922.

Argentina had won the two previous tournaments but withdrew in 1949. Brazil were rampant, scoring 39 goals in their seven first-phase games. They beat Ecuador 9-1, Bolivia 10-1, Peru 7-1 and, most satisfying, Uruguay 5-1 in Rio before 45,000 ecstatic fans. In the final they beat Paraguay, who had beaten them earlier in the series, by seven goals. Such a performance only served to add to Brazil's confidence in believing they had a date with destiny in 1950.

The third World Cup was supposed to have 16 nations competing but only 13 turned up. It was still an arduous task to get to South America and the cost was significant.

Argentina pulled out, prolonging their disagreement with the Brazilian football authorities, and Czechoslovakia stayed at home, possibly due to economic and political reasons. France were invited but after realising they had a relatively weak side, they looked at the draw and decided they would be better off declining. This was, though, England's first World Cup and they were named joint favourites along with Brazil. Italy, the holders, were also highly fancied as were Argentina until they withdrew. Scotland could also have been there as FIFA had allocated two places from their group but the Scots made clear they could not travel if they had not won the all-United Kingdom qualifying section. India, who had qualified by default due to mass withdrawals in their region, withdrew.

Brazilian football had been transformed by the emergence of black players and the game had played its part in creating a national identity. It has been said, down the decades, that Brazil only really comes together as a nation for football, and in particular, the World Cup. In the beginning, football was only played by white Brazilians and foreigners. Black people were not permitted to play. As the game grew the barriers came down, and soon the country's intelligentsia, notably sociologists and politicians, identified Brazil's mixed-race heritage as a huge positive that could create a more creative style of football that was a compelling alternative to the technical European style. It was the beginning of the fabled *o jogo bonito* – the beautiful game. Black players would characterise the Brazilian approach to the 1950 World Cup.

The Vasco da Gama club from Rio de Janeiro had a strong influence on the Brazilian national team. There was no national football championship in Brazil at the time, so the state championships were the main source of competition. Vasco were the champions of Rio state, a powerful league that included Fluminense, Flamengo and Botafogo, not to mention Bangu. Vasco provided eight players for the 1950 squad, including goalkeeper Moacir Barbosa, Augusto, Danilo, Ademir de Menezes and Chico. When Vasco went through the 1949 state championship unbeaten, Ademir scored 30 goals in the league.

Ademir was a terrifying player whose imposing jaw and physical appearance would intimidate defenders. He was not only strong but his pace caused the opposition to panic, especially when he would suddenly switch gears. Ademir went on to win the golden boot at the 1950 World Cup but he was just one of several fearsome strikers available to Brazil's manager, Flávio Costa, who was also Vasco da Gama's coach between 1947 and 1950.

One of the jewels in Brazil's crown was Zizinho, an experienced attacking midfielder who was sold by Flamengo, against his will, to Bangu in 1950. Zizinho could do anything with the ball and had a vast array of skills. Pelé, who was still a small boy in 1950, claimed that he was his hero and 'the complete player'. Certainly, before Pelé's own era, the Rio-born Zizinho was considered the best Brazilian player of all time.

Zizinho was injured before the World Cup got under way and missed the first two group games. His place was taken by the robust Baltazar of Corinthians, but once Zizinho was fit, 'Golden head' – as he was known – could not win a place in the team again. Chico was another Vasco forward to catch the eye, an athletic, two-footed dribbler who had an excellent scoring record for his club.

Jair of Palmeiras was an outstanding winger whose technical ability worried defenders. His flamboyant skill was one of the highlights of the World Cup. Jair was heartbroken by Brazil's defeat in 1950 but was credited with helping an emerging talent, none other than Pelé, to develop during his time at Santos.

The squad of Ademir, Zizinho, Jair and Chico produced a brand of football that few had seen before. Brian Glanville, in his history of the World Cup, said Brazil had played 'football of the future, almost surreal' which was technically superb but 'tactically unexceptional'.

Their warm-up games didn't provide any hint of what was to come. In a match with Flamengo in the work-in-progress Maracanã, the 3,000 workmen still frantically trying to finish the stadium (they wouldn't get the job done until 1965), were cheering on the Rio team who had impressed them more than the national side.

However, the international press felt Brazil's home advantage would give the locals an interesting and satisfying tournament and predicted their brilliant speed and dash would win the title against either England or Italy. Back in London, the newspapers were insistent England were warm favourites in their first World Cup. There was little mention of Uruguay as contenders.

When the competition kicked off, the Maracanã was still not entirely finished due to delays and over-spending issues. It was more or less fit for purpose just seven days before the World Cup was due to start. However, there were still no proper toilets and the paint was barely dry. The site was 190,000 square metres in size and had accounted for 80,000 square metres of concrete, some of the first ever manufactured in Brazil. Work began in 1948 and around 10,000 people were employed. Bizarrely, 90 per cent of the competition's budget was spent on the stadium.

Although some political groups still pondered over the logic of hosting a major sporting event when so many people were struggling to feed themselves, momentum was building in getting the nation behind the *Seleção*. The song of the World Cup, 'Marcha do Scratch Brasileiro', was composed by Lamartine Babo and sung by Sílvio Caldo, '*Eu sou brasileiro, tu es brasileiro. Vamos torcer com fé*' – 'I am Brazilian, you are Brazilian, let's support our team with faith.' In 1950, that faith was almost totally – at 93.4 per cent – Roman Catholic.

Enthusiasm was at fever pitch as Brazil kicked off their campaign in the Maracanã against Mexico on 24 June. Over 80,000 were in the stadium, around half of the capacity. The Mexicans had a fairly comfortable path to Rio, disposing of the United States and Cuba in the qualifiers. Birds were released, balloons soared into the Rio sky and there was a noisy gun salute and leaflets dropped on to the crowd by aeroplane. This was all aimed at building fervour among Brazil's fans. Mexico strolled out 15 minutes late and their inexperience showed as they were beaten 4-0 by the hosts.

It was a fairly dull affair but good enough to kick-start the competition. The following day, Brazil's group rivals Yugoslavia and Switzerland met in Belo Horizonte with the former winning 3-0. Holders Italy were beaten by the Swedes and England started with a 2-0 victory against Chile. The Yugoslavs worried Brazil, though, as they had some excellent players and knew how to score goals, as their 4-1 win against Mexico demonstrated. While they were stamping their credentials on the World Cup, Brazil were rather clumsily being held 2-2 by the unfancied Swiss. Brazil had to win their group to qualify for the final round, an unusual four-team round robin comprising the group winners. Brazil held second place going into the final group game, so a draw would be enough for Yugoslavia and end their interest, which would spell disaster for the home nation and FIFA.

Interestingly, the final games in group A were staggered over two days, unlike the other groups. Brazil won 2-0 with goals from Zizinho and Ademir, playing much better and more fluid football than in the draw with Switzerland. It was enough to send them through to the final group. Meanwhile, Italy had been knocked out at the hands of Sweden, and Uruguay had won through to the final section. England would fail miserably, losing to the USA and Spain. Only on return to the United Kingdom did the English realise that their coaching and approach to the game needed modifying, but it would take another setback, in 1953, before they truly took notice.

Some newspapers couldn't help but snipe at the quality of the remaining teams, notably the Argentinian *La Razón* which noted that four teams were left in the World Cup but in no way did they represent the best in football. The newspaper was, of course, referring to its own national team's self-imposed absence.

Brazil really came alive in the final group, playing wonderful, fast-flowing football that gave their opponents no chance – in front of huge six-figure crowds. The first games saw Uruguay and Spain draw 2-2 and Brazil totally dismantle Sweden 7-1. So impressive was Brazil's forward line of Ademir, Jair, Chico and Zizinho that two-time World Cup winner Vittorio Pozzo, manager of Italy, claimed the *Seleção* were the best team after earlier admitting he was unmoved by their play. His reaction was echoed in the Italian media, who applauded the sheer artistry of players like Zizinho. Sweden were no fools, so a 7-1 victory was a major achievement and when Brazil won 6-1 against Spain, there wasn't a single person across the country who didn't feel the World Cup would be won by the hosts on 16 July.

Only coach Flavió Costa refused to take it for granted. Everywhere there were signs that Brazil just might have been a little over-confident of securing the single point they needed from their final match with Uruguay. The press didn't help, pre-printing their front covers for the day after the game with proclamations of glory. *O Mundo* was among them, creating a lavish edition with 'These are the champions' emblazoned across the columns with a picture of the team.

In Montevideo, aeroplanes took off with Uruguay 6 Brazil 0 daubed on them. Their team was seen as merely making up the numbers on Brazil's big day. How wrong the masses were, for Brazil were left distraught, a little red-faced and their self-esteem battered by the outcome.

Everybody in Brazil wanted to see the game. They queued for hours for tickets, the unlucky applicants becoming violent when they were turned away empty-handed. They went on the rampage in downtown Rio, smashing huge plate glass windows of major department stores. On the day, fans found their way into the Maracanã without tickets and the estimated crowd was more like 200,000 than the official 174,000 paying attendance.

The score was level at half-time, 0-0. This was enough for Brazil to be champions, and when Friaça of São Paulo put them ahead in the 47th minute with a goal that was hotly disputed by Uruguay's captain Obdulio Varela, it looked to be over for the 1930 winners.

Then came the first of two disastrous blows for the Brazilians. Less than 20 minutes after Friaça's goal, Alcides Ghiggia, on the right, outpaced Bigode and crossed for Juan Schiaffino to send an angled shot high into the net. The silence in the Maracanã was deafening, the eeriness scaring Costa's players and unsettling them for the rest of the game. Still, a draw would do it for Brazil.

But with 11 minutes to go, silence turned to sheer horror as Uruguay scored again. Ghiggia passed to Julio Pérez and he gratefully accepted the return ball behind Bigode. This time he sent a bobbling shot to the near post, which deceived goalkeeper Barbosa and found the back of the net. More silence, accompanied by tears, heads in hands and disbelief. At the whistle, a feeling of doom prevailed as the crowd, stunned that their heroes had failed to deliver, stood watching Uruguay's players celebrate their unexpected victory.

Nobody had seriously anticipated that the best team in the world could be beaten in their iconic and magnificent stadium. Jules Rimet handed the cup to Varela and quickly left the scene, which by now had become chaotic. Brazil's players had long run for cover and took their guilt and anguish away from the stadium. Some, such as Barbosa, 'the man who made Brazil cry', never got over the defeat. He was certainly never forgiven for that second goal. Old tensions came to the surface – the three black players, Barbosa, Juvenal and Bigode, were all blamed for the defeat. Zizinho, arguably the best player in the world at the time, would spend the rest of his life taking his telephone off the hook on 16 July, the anniversary of the final.

In the streets of Rio and other cities, violence broke out, resulting in the army, navy and air force having to back up the police. 'We are a luckless people,' said one headline. 'A nation deprived of joy.' So desperate were they to look for clues that Brazil consigned their white and blue kit to the dustbin, creating a new, dynamic and forward-looking yellow, blue and green strip, the one everyone now recognises as quintessentially Brazilian.

They would have their time, but the disaster that was *Maracanazo* has never been allowed to pass from memory. In 2014 they had their chance to bury the ghost of 1950, but they didn't take it. Will they ever get the chance?

7

Hungary 1954: And the world wept

IF EVER there was a football stadium that induced fear among visiting teams it was surely the Nép, the people's stadium in the heart of Budapest's 14th district. It's now known as the Ferenc Puskás Stadium and bears little, if any, resemblance to the vast communist bowl that was erected in 1953.

Before it became a modern-day tribute to Hungary's greatest ever footballer, the Nép had become a sorry sight – a crumbling reminder of a time when the Hungarians were the finest team on the planet. The scale of the stadium was still there to be seen, its exterior including caverns beneath the stands that would surely have told a tale or two if they had the chance. All around Budapest, there are little mementoes of Hungary's brilliant team of the early 1950s, the 'Mighty Magyars', who pointed the way to a new, exciting future for a game that was still stuck in a pre-Second World War paradigm.

In a side street in the charming Hungarian capital, a car park is adorned with images from Hungary's memorable victory at Wembley in November 1953. Outside the Nép there were monuments to Hungarian internationals, socialist statues depicting the vitality of sportsmen and women and in a humdrum neighbourhood, an old man sits in a cafe called 3:6

that is adorned with pictures of the golden team – a cafe that was once owned by a member of that famous group, Nándor Hidegkuti.

There's nobody left from that team and Hungarian football is now something of a backwater, despite attempts by the government and the controversial Victor Orbán to kick-start the revival of the game in Budapest and beyond. It's a tragedy, because the Hungarians laid the foundations for modern football and should have become world champions in 1954.

Like the Dutch in 1974, Hungary of 20 years earlier are frequently named as the best team never to win the World Cup. Anyone keen on conspiracy theories might put that down to the era in which they went so close to being crowned the best – the Cold War. At the time, there was genuine hatred and suspicion of anyone or anything from behind or aligned to the iron curtain. Although it has rarely been suggested, a communist world champion would have been a shot in the arm for communism, socialism and the Soviets.

It is often forgotten that Hungary also reached the World Cup Final in 1938, losing to a strong and intimidating Italian side who had won the 1934 competition. Hungary ran Italy close but were beaten 4-2 in Paris. Their captain was György Sárosi of Ferencváros, one of Europe's top players in the interwar years. Hungary's influence on the development of the global game was unequivocal, providing a stream of coaches who almost acted as sporting missionaries. In Italy, around 50 Hungarian coaches were hired across the 1920s and 1930s. The Hungarians were also involved in the rise of pan-European club football, notably the Mitropa Cup which was introduced in the late 1920s and saw four winners from Hungary (Ferencváros and Újpest twice each).

Budapest was a footballing hotbed in the late 1930s and central Europe was where it was all happening in the evolution of the professional game. It was out of this potpourri of intellectuals, progressive coaches and ambitious sportsmen that Hungary's football clubs formed much of their identity: Vasas, the club of the iron and steel workers; MTK, formed and favoured by aristocrats and Jews but later the club of the secret police; Kispest, who later became the Hungarian army team; Újpest, a general sports club that was the club of the police; and Ferencváros, a club from the ninth district that was generally out of favour with the postwar administration due to its right-wing history.

The flag-wavers for a new type of football were a trio of coaches: Márton Bukovi, Béla Guttmann and Gusztáv Sebes. In 1948, Sebes, along with Béla Mandik and Gábor Kompóti-Kléber, formed a three-man committee to manage the Hungarian national team.

Sebes was an admirer of the Austrian *Wunderteam* and the Italian World Cup winners of 1934 and 1938, both of whom had been built around a core from one club side. It was his intention to attempt a 'club' approach and he decided upon the Kispest team. This club became aligned to the army and was renamed Honvéd, enabling them to recruit players who had been conscripted into the military, hence they signed Sándor Kocsis, Zoltán Czibor and László Budai from Ferencváros along with other stars from Budapest clubs.

Sebes was able to use Honvéd as a quasi-national team training camp, which didn't go down too well with the other top Hungarian clubs. Újpest won the first four Hungarian titles, but Honvéd and MTK, who became Red Banner (Vörös Lobogó), were the dominant forces thereafter.

Hungary were among several national teams to withdraw from the 1950 World Cup, so the first glimpse of their footballing prowess had to wait until the 1952 Olympics. Held in Helsinki, this was the Olympics of Emil Zátopek, the Czech long-distance runner. But the Hungarian football team was also among the stars of the Games. They arrived in Helsinki unbeaten for two years, although most of their successes were against Eastern bloc states. They rarely ventured out of their comfort zone and this prompted some critics to question whether their reputation had been truly earned.

There's no denying that the first flickers of the golden team, or at least global awareness of them, came in Finland where they started the tournament as joint favourites with the USSR. They comfortably beat Romania, Italy, Turkey and Sweden to reach the final, scoring 18 goals on the way and conceding two. Sir Stanley Rous, the president of the Football Association, was so impressed when he saw Hungary wallop Sweden 6-0 that he invited Sebes to bring a team to England. Little did Rous know it, but that conversation would effectively make football history.

In the Olympic final they didn't perform up to their high standards, but still had enough to beat Yugoslavia 2-0 with goals from the 25-year-old Ferenc Puskás and Zoltán Czibor. Yugoslavia were clearly expecting worse, for they were so relieved when Puskás missed a penalty that their players rushed to kiss him on both cheeks! Years later, he recalled the emotion that greeted the Olympic success: 'On the journey home, the train kept stopping at every station to allow crowds to greet us. The scenes at [Budapest] Keleti station were unbelievable. There were around 100,000 people crammed into the surrounding streets to celebrate. We were ecstatic, that was our first great victory and our hearts were still so young.'

Puskás had been playing senior football for more than eight years by the time he appeared in the Olympics. He made his debut for Kispest as a 16-year-old in December 1943 and by 1945/46 he was the Hungarian league's top scorer, netting 36 goals in 34 games. He made his international debut in August 1945 against Austria, scoring as Hungary won 5-2. Puskás became a goal machine for Kispest and, after the army took over, Honvéd. He was given the rank of major by the Hungarian ministry of defence and this earned him the nickname 'the Galloping Major'.

Hungary's performance in Helsinki had opened people's eyes, but it was nothing compared to the seismic effect of the game in London in 1953. England were unbeaten by a foreign country on their own soil and although their initial foray into the World Cup in Brazil in 1950 had ended in humiliation, including a 1-0 defeat against the USA, there was still a reluctance to admit it was possible England were no longer the best in the world.

Hungary's reputation had been germinating through word of mouth, along with their impressive record. But they were a team from a mysterious part of Europe and consequently viewed with as much curiosity as if they had just landed in a spaceship from Mars. Wembley was a sell-out, which was impressive given the game was to be played on a foggy November afternoon in midweek. 'No game in the past 25 years has captured the imagination so much,' said one newspaper in previewing the contest.

Hungary were being billed by the *Daily Mirror* as the champions of Europe, 'An outstanding world-class team of highly charged athletes, superb individual ball players and a beautifully disciplined crew.' The media were fully aware of the challenge ahead for the home team, but worried hacks urged the public to 'trust the England knack', while Bernard Joy, an old-time amateur figure who played for Arsenal in his younger days, insisted the answer to continental ball skills was good old-fashioned English tackling. Others hoped the physical approach of England would knock Hungary out of their stride.

Joy was not shy of putting his patriotism on display, noting that a Hungarian victory would prompt the communists to claim it was an endorsement for their way of life which epitomised the people's democracy. 'For that reason, I am more anxious that we should win this game than any other since the clash with Germany in Berlin in 1938,' he admitted.

A few journalists were also critical of the Hungarian definition of sporting amateurs, which they claimed their players were. They referred to the team as 'government amateurs', adding that although they might be soldiers in name, they were in fact 100 per cent sportsmen.

Puskás, the focus of attention from the public and press alike, was confident Hungary were in London for one reason. 'We are going to win, we wouldn't have come here if we thought we were going to lose,' he said. But it wasn't all one way, by any means. Hungary, while exuding confidence, also feared individuals such as Stanley Matthews. Although Puskás demonstrated that he was a supremely gifted individual, the very culture of Hungary's football was based on the concept of 'the team', a coda that Sebes called 'socialist football'. But so concerned were Sebes and his team that he spent a fortnight preparing for the game by training on sodden pitches with an English-style ball.

The preparation was meticulous and paved the way for one of the most influential 90-minute games in football history, certainly in Great Britain. Furthermore, it highlighted that Hungary were a brilliant team packed with virtuosity and intelligence. It was a grey winter's afternoon at Wembley and England were torn apart by a team possessing devastating pace, sublime skill and powerful finishing ability. Hungary produced ten shots on goal to every English attempt. They went a goal ahead after one minute and with less than half an hour gone, Hungary were 4-1 up. It was embarrassing for England and their leaden-footed team. The final score was 6-3, the highlight being a piece of trickery from Puskás, dragging the ball away from defender Billy Wright and leaving the stricken England skipper sprawling on the floor.

Puskás was only one star performer of many that day. Nándor Hidegkuti, a few years older than the major, was playing in the so-called deep-lying centre-forward role, presenting a foretaste of the future of the game that has morphed into what we now call the modern number ten. Hidegkuti scored a hat-trick at Wembley and was one of the reasons why a well-known commentator declared that the crowd had seen 'football dressed in new colours with something we have not seen before in this country'. Hungary sent shock waves rolling through English football, with experts calling for change and urging the sport to wake up to a new future. That future manifested itself in the end of the old W-M formation and the rise of a more flexible 4-2-4 system.

Hungary revelled in their success and proved it was no fluke when they beat England 7-1 in Budapest a few months later in their last game before the 1954 World Cup. It wasn't just the style of play that set them apart from the English – the Hungarians' boots were more lightweight, their shirts more slimline. For years, England's players had resembled men in heavy armour rather than sportsmen when they ran out on to the pitch. Centre-half Syd Owen of Luton Town summed up the difference between the two teams after the game in the Nép, 'I have never seen anything like it; they were like men from another planet.'

If that was the case, Hungary were poised to capture the world in the summer of 1954 in Switzerland. This was supposed to be their World Cup, their official coronation as the kings of world football, and for much of the tournament, it looked a likely outcome.

They certainly went into the World Cup highly confident. In their group they were drawn against South Korea and West Germany. They beat South Korea 9-0 in their first game, with Puskás and Sándor Kocsis scoring five between them. Then came the clash with West Germany, who were making their first appearance in the competition since the war. Nobody expected the Germans to win the World Cup in 1954, although they did possess some fine players, notably the dashing Fritz Walter of Kaiserslautern.

If there was a flaw in the Hungarian side then it was their gung-ho approach. They were supremely skilful, highly energetic and very individual but there were rumours that Puskás didn't get on with everyone in the team, especially his colleagues in the forward line.

Hungary thrashed West Germany 8-3 in Basel. They simply ran the Germans into the ground. But Sepp Herberger, their coach, proved to be as canny as his successors in the dugout. He gambled on fielding a slightly weakened side to avoid showing his full hand, although not as under-strength as people have subsequently made out. The peculiar structure to the competition meant that in four-team groups, only two games per team were played and Germany had won their other match by putting four past Turkey. They would qualify by beating Turkey again in a play-off, 7-2.

But the key incident in Hungary's dismantling of West Germany was a foul by Werner Liebrich on Puskás. It sidelined him for an hour and was later revealed to be a hairline fracture of the ankle. Puskás was adamant that it was deliberately designed to put him out of the competition. He later described it as 'a vicious kick in the back of my ankle when I was no longer playing the ball'. Fritz Walter, when asked about the tackle, merely said, 'He [Puskás] landed awkwardly.'

Liebrich, like Walter, played for Kaiserslautern. He was a member of the club's title-winning teams of 1951 and 1952 and was renowned for being a little over-zealous in his approach to the game. In 1950 he had turned down AC Milan to remain in Germany, so he was a sought-after defender. The state of the Puskás ankle would make national news in Hungary; it was monitored like no other ankle in history.

Puskás, whose ankle ligaments were almost severed, missed the quarter-final against Brazil – the notorious 'Battle of Berne' which saw Hungary win 4-2. The game was a catalogue of fouls, off-the-ball antics and petulance, much of which was blamed on the Brazilians. 'They were like animals, it was a disgrace, a horrible match,' said referee Arthur Ellis afterwards. Hungary's victory was finally clinched by a header from Kocsis, 'the Golden Head', who made the scoreline 4-2 in the 88th minute.

Puskás watched from the side and allegedly became embroiled in the post-match turmoil which included a punch-up, flying bottles and a dressing room invasion. Hungary were so incensed by the behaviour of Brazil they cancelled a tour of the country. Others were critical of both, saying two of the best football teams in the world destroyed their own artistry through cruel tackling and sly jabs.

Puskás also missed the semi-final win against Uruguay, which was a brilliant and gruelling encounter that went into extra time but was secured, once more, by two headers from Kocsis. It was another 4-2 win for the Magyars, and so well-matched were the two teams that Hungary believed they had faced the best side they had ever come up against. Even today, the Hungary versus Uruguay game is considered one of the great all-time World Cup fixtures, full of technical excellence. But Hungary, having won through against two top South American opponents, had a race on their hands to get their star player fit.

Hungary's opponents in the final were West Germany, the team they had demolished in the group stage. The only stumbling block, aside from Puskás' fitness, was the fact the German side was markedly different from the one that had been beaten 8-3 in Basel 14 days earlier. Only five members of that team lined up in Berne's Wankdorf Stadium for the final.

Puskás, due to his influence on Sebes, was deemed fit enough to play, but to accommodate him the Hungarian team had to be reshaped. The popular Laszlo Budai had played well in the previous rounds but he was dropped to make way for Puskás. It didn't seem to matter, as Hungary went into a 2-0 lead with Puskás scoring after six minutes and Zoltán Czibor adding another two minutes later. But as the game wore on Puskás became less effective and his ankle slowed him down. Rumours abounded that he insisted on playing, despite his lack of fitness. He was so confident Hungary would win that he felt that even though he might be below par it would be enough.

Despite enjoying 90 per cent of the possession, Hungary appeared over-confident and a little jaded; the effort needed to dispose of Brazil and Uruguay had clearly taken its toll. In addition, the Germans arguably built their renowned reputation for resilience and unflinching commitment in this game and drew level with goals from Max Morlock on ten minutes and Helmut Rahn on 18.

Six minutes from the end, Rahn added a third for West Germany, sending a low drive past goalkeeper Gyula Grosics. Hungary were behind for the first time but they kept going and Puskás had a late shot ruled out for offside. Even in the final seconds, Czibor was denied by German keeper Toni Turek. The final score, 3-2 to West Germany, was seen as a landmark following the Second World War. The 'Miracle of Berne' has become part of German folklore. Hungary's defeat, however, is often referred to as a catalyst for the uprising of 1956.

In true Orwellian fashion, there was a search for scapegoats. The team had to be smuggled into Budapest under armed guard for fear of violence directed at them. Thousands of people protested in Budapest's poorer districts, angry the golden team that had lit up the postwar years had failed. The streets, which had been festooned with bunting in anticipation of victory, were soon stripped of all their decorations.

Some people laid the blame for defeat on an arrogant Puskás and abused him when he returned to Hungary. The regime, interpreting the loss as a defeat for the state, targeted goalkeeper Grosics, who was arrested and charged with smuggling goods and involving himself in espionage, perhaps as a little payback for attempting to defect a few years earlier.

Sebes, meanwhile, kept his job for a while but was later denounced by Ministry of Sport officials for being too bourgeois. He often claimed that if Hungary had won the World Cup, there would have been no counter-revolution in 1956 but a powerful thrust in the building of socialism across the country. Such was the need for someone to blame that in Budapest, hundreds of inebriated and angry fans stormed the national radio station and shouted for radio commentator Gyorgy Szepes to be dragged out.

Puskás, some years later, accused the Germans of being doped and a study by the University of Leipzig claimed their players may have been injected with methamphetamine, a drug that is often used today to treat attention deficit hyperactivity disorder.

Hungarian hearts were broken on that June afternoon and chin-stroking intellectuals have often tried to fathom out why the best football team in the world fell apart after being in such a commanding position so early on in the final. There have even been some conspiracy theories suggesting it was all an anti-communist plot, that the world didn't really want an iron curtain country to win the competition.

It was a cold war in those grey post-Second World War years, but the team in red shirts was very hot indeed. Those who admired pure football played by magical artists with such a swagger wept about the thwarted glory of Hungary. By 1956, the dream of the golden team was over as the country descended into political chaos; Puskás and others footballers who were on a tour at the time with Honvéd found themselves exiled. Puskás, of course, had a second wind at Real Madrid but Hungary's national team – after one defeat in 43 games – is yet to scale such heights again.

8

Burnley 1962: Homegrown heroes run out of steam

WHEN BURNLEY won the Football League in 1960, it was achieved with a largely home-spun team comprising youngsters who graduated through the club's youth system and created a dynamic group of players who entertained and became very popular. Of the title-winning line-up, half came directly through the club's network, others were signed from non-league football and only Alex Elder and Jimmy McIlroy cost transfer fees. Over in Manchester, Matt Busby's Manchester United had shown how youth development could yield significant results in the mid-1950s, but little Burnley, from a homely town perched close to the moors, provided an example of how it could be done in less grandiose surroundings.

While United had Busby, Burnley were guided by their pugnacious and somewhat confrontational chairman, Bob Lord. He was a local butcher, the epitome of the working-class lad made good, and extremely passionate about Burnley Football Club. Lord was born in Burnley in 1908 and was a Freemason. Despite his somewhat 'local' appearance, he was also innovative and willing to push boundaries. In 1951 he joined the board at the club. This came after Lord bid for a 79-acre piece of land at Home Farm, Gawthorpe Hall, with the aim of establishing an academy for the development of young players. He paid around £5,000 for the site, more than he originally anticipated, and by the time the club's annual general meeting took place he had built up a major shareholding in Burnley. In 1955, at the age of 47, he was named chairman, fulfilling a lifelong ambition.

Lord's Burnley enjoyed four seasons in which they were on the fringe of the championship race, finishing seventh three times and sixth. When Lord took over, Alan Brown, a former player in the 1940s, was already running the team, but in 1957 Billy Dougall, a Scottish left-half who had appeared for Burnley in the late 1920s, was in charge. Dougall was a key figure in the club's burgeoning youth programme, but in January 1958 he resigned. Lord moved quickly to persuade old favourite Harry Potts to become manager.

Potts, a deep-thinking man, had been a member of Burnley's 1946/47 team that won promotion to the First Division and finished runners-up in the FA Cup. His playing career ended in 1956 with Everton, so he was relatively young for a manager. An unassuming fellow who rarely courted the spotlight, Potts became one of the most highly respected managers in the game, often mentioned in the same breath as Bill Nicholson, Stan Cullis and Bill Shankly. He was an advocate of the new 4-4-2 formation.

Burnley benefitted from a conveyor belt of young talent. 'We hit a purple patch, getting a lot of young players from the north-east and Scotland and Northern Ireland,' said Jimmy McIlroy when recalling those memorable years at Burnley. The heady mix of youth and experience proved to be a huge success. John Connelly, who would become part of the England 1966 squad, later highlighted the team's strengths, 'We had a brilliant blend, but Mac [McIlroy] stood out, of course.'

McIlroy joined Burnley in 1950 from Glentoran, costing £7,000 in a deal that became slightly controversial as the Irish club claimed Burnley had made an illegal approach to the player. He won 55 caps for Northern Ireland and became one of his country's greatest footballers, a composed passer of the ball and the brains of the team. He stayed with Burnley for 13 years, eventually falling out with Lord. McIlroy later commented, 'He was the sort of person you needed on your side. He did a lot of good, but he could have been nice and shown a more gentle side.' In 1963 McIlroy was sold to Stoke City to team up with Stanley Matthews, a decision that incensed many Burnley fans who had always given the popular Irishman the benefit of the doubt.

McIlroy was a pivotal figure in Burnley's 1960 title-winning team. They didn't top the league table until the very final game, although they were chasing the front two for much of the campaign. They won seven of their first ten matches, leaving them in fourth place with a cluster of clubs, and one point behind leaders Tottenham. In November they beat reigning champions Wolverhampton Wanderers 4-1 at Turf Moor, a result that confirmed the potential of Potts's team. Burnley went into 1960 in third place but had seen their hopes damaged by a 4-1 home defeat against Manchester United, just two days after they had won 2-1 at Old Trafford.

When Burnley beat Tottenham 2-0 in March the media enthused about the exuberance of their young side, who were now chasing a league and cup double. But when the Clarets went to Wolves at the end of the month they were four points behind leaders Spurs, albeit with two games in hand. Wolves gained revenge for their earlier drubbing by hammering Burnley 6-1. Doubts started to creep in.

With two matches left Burnley were level on points with Wolves, who had just one to play. The title was within their grasp. On the final day of the campaign, Wolves won 5-1 at Chelsea while Burnley drew, nervously, with Fulham at home. That pushed Burnley down to third place, one point behind

Wolves and level with Spurs. But Burnley still had to visit Manchester City on 2 May and a win would give them their first championship since 1921.

Winger Brian Pilkington, who arrived at Burnley via Leyland Motors, gave them a fourth-minute lead, but City equalised in the 12th minute. Trevor Meredith, just 20 and 5ft 5in tall, volleyed the winner after a defensive error after half an hour. Burnley won 2-1 and lifted the second title in their history with a team built mostly from within.

In 1960/61 Tottenham stole the limelight and Burnley had to settle for fourth place, even though they did beat Spurs 4-2 at home and drew 4-4 at White Hart Lane. In the FA Cup, Spurs overcame Burnley in the semi-final and went on to complete the double. Nevertheless, Burnley's setup was still the envy of the rest of English football and international selectors were already recognising the likes of John Angus, Brian Miller, John Connelly, Ray Pointer and Brian Pilkington. Some pundits were so impressed with Burnley that they predicted their young team could become 'the team of the '60s'. A similar sentiment was expressed by Bob Lord on more than one occasion.

Burnley's squad changed little for the 1961/62 season; they were still young and full of energy and many considered them among the favourites for honours. Tottenham, a team that the press and fans eulogised about for years, were also seen as possible champions, although they had the welcome distraction of the European Cup. Meanwhile, a rustic team from Suffolk, Ipswich Town, arrived in the First Division after winning promotion under their taciturn manager Alf Ramsey. Other clubs, such as Manchester United, Arsenal and Everton, were in transition.

After the opening game, at Arsenal, Burnley were tipped to be a force again. They drew 2-2 at Highbury and impressed with their methodical approach. There were over 40,000 at Arsenal but the newspapers noticed that crowds were on the decline. Burnley's stock was in the ascendancy once more, though, and they put on a spectacular show in their first home game of the campaign as they beat Ipswich 4-3. Although Burnley, to quote one report, 'looked like a champion side', the plaudits went to newly promoted Ipswich. Burnley had 33 shots to Ipswich's 12 and put on such a display that the 24,000 crowd cheered both sides off the pitch. 'They all played like £100-a-week men,' said one scribe.

This was a reference to the ongoing battle between football and the Professional Footballers' Association (PFA), who had been championing the abolition of the maximum wage. Bob Lord was among those who eventually called for the removal of any wage ceiling. Johnny Haynes of Fulham became the Football League's first £100-a-week player.

After beating Bolton, though, Burnley had something of a rude awakening a week later when Ipswich ran riot at Portman Road, defeating them 6-2 in the return game. Ipswich had only earned one point from their first three games but they tore Burnley apart. 'Burnley's chairman, Bob Lord, must have chewed up his cigar to see the team he loves walking off at the end like a boxer who has taken 15 rounds of punishment and doesn't know the result,' reported the *Herald*.

Burnley went top of the table on 9 September after beating West Bromwich Albion 3-1 at Turf Moor. They were the third team to hit the summit – Sheffield Wednesday and Manchester City were the others – and the general consensus was that the 1961/62 title race would be a tight one. At that point, only three points separated Burnley from Bolton Wanderers in eighth place.

In the space of a week, however, Burnley unequivocally displayed their championship credentials with two emphatic victories in the Midlands. At Birmingham's St Andrew's, Burnley won 6-2 and totally outclassed their hosts, leaving admiring home spectators claiming they were the best team in the league. The locals were so taken with Burnley's open, attacking style that some predicted they could lead a much-needed renaissance in the English game. Certainly, the form of Pointer, Connelly, Miller and Harris was catching the eye, notably the opportunism of Pointer, who won a call-up to the England team for the World Cup game with Luxembourg. If that result wasn't sensational enough, Burnley repeated the scoreline at Leicester City a few days later, scoring four goals in a 14-minute first-half spell. Leading 4-1 at half-time, thanks to their blistering pace and constant waves of attack, Burnley put six goals past England's future World Cup-winning keeper, Gordon Banks.

Another foretaste of the future was seen at Burnley's next game at Turf Moor when Everton were the visitors. Burnley went two goals ahead and their goalkeeper, Adam Blacklaw, was hit by bottles thrown by Everton fans. Fireworks were let off and police had to break up scuffles on the terraces. It would not be too long before such scenes were regular events at matches in Britain. Burnley also made the wrong headlines when Bob Lord was rebuked by the Football League for fielding a weakened team towards the end of the 1960/61 season. Lord, described as having a 'sandpaper personality', was accused of shoving the club into the face of the public and one reporter, Frank McGhee, while praising a brilliant Burnley side, added that they were nearly as good as Lord believed them to be.

All eyes were on Lord when Burnley went to Fulham's Craven Cottage and came away with a 5-3 victory. Lord – 'the man they're trying to gag' – sat puffing on his trademark cigar and his red face beamed as Fulham were overcome by a Connelly hat-trick and an excellent performance by Pointer, who had disappointed in his England debut. Walter Winterbottom was in the stand watching and saw enough to recall Pointer for the next international squad. Johnny

Haynes, another England international and a Fulham legend, commented that his team had been outplayed by the best side he had seen in 1961/62.

Without doubt, Burnley had upstaged the previous year's media darlings, Tottenham, who were languishing in seventh place and had already lost three of their first ten games. Burnley were top, four points ahead of West Ham and shaping up as title favourites even at this early stage of the season. Their youthful vigour and attacking play contrasted with a Spurs team that had seemingly lost some of its self-confidence – perhaps the task of winning both the league and cup had finally caught up on Bill Nicholson's team?

There was no lack of confidence at Burnley but shorn of Pointer and Connelly, who were on England duty, they could have postponed their table-topping clash with West Ham at Upton Park. They chose not to and regretted it as the Hammers raced into a two-goal lead. Burnley pulled one back, but they were beaten for only the second time in the league.

That defeat seemed to knock Burnley's self-esteem and a fortnight later, they received another setback in London. Visiting Tottenham, who had now regained some of their verve, this game was something of a clash of the giants, the undisputed champions of 1961 against a team that had won the title in 1960 and wanted to recapture their crown in 1962. Spurs made some changes to their regular line-up, bringing 18-year-old Frank Saul and Eddie Clayton into their forward line. Both made a difference, but Burnley went into a 2-0 lead inside 14 minutes at White Hart Lane with both goals coming from Pointer. By half-time, however, Tottenham had turned things around and led 3-2 before a late strike from Cliff Jones gave them a comprehensive victory. Burnley were still leading and had a three-point advantage over the reigning champions, who were now second, but it was clear Spurs were not letting their crown go without a fight.

Another defeat, at Nottingham Forest, further opened up the title race. Burnley were at the front, three points ahead of Everton, West Ham and Tottenham, who were all on 20 points. Spurs strengthened their case by signing Jimmy Greaves from AC Milan. Greaves, who had left Chelsea in the summer, had endured an unhappy time in Italy and opted to join the north London club as opposed to his old employers, who were languishing at the foot of the First Division. Spurs would have to wait for his league debut owing to international clearance and the return of Greaves's fitness.

Burnley slipped up again at home to Wolves, drawing 3-3, while Ipswich came into view after beating Manchester United 4-1. A week later, on 25 November, Burnley repeated that scoreline, winning at Old Trafford and extending their lead to three points again. Ipswich were in dogged pursuit of top place, though, with everyone expecting them to lose momentum. Burnley opened up a five-point lead a few days later as they won 2-1 at Chelsea and Ipswich were beaten 3-0 at Aston Villa.

On Boxing Day, Burnley bounced back with a 4-0 win against Sheffield Wednesday but the most ominous development was the debut of Greaves at Spurs. He netted a hat-trick as his new club beat Blackpool 5-2. Suddenly, the championship looked a little tougher for Burnley.

The FA Cup arrived and Burnley were declared favourites. They easily overcame Queens Park Rangers in the third round, scoring six goals. By mid-January Burnley were two points clear in the league and had two games in hand after beating Manchester City 6-3, while Spurs had crept into second place and Ipswich were still upsetting the form book in third.

Burnley were fortunate to gain a draw at West Bromwich Albion after spending much of their time defending, and in the next round of the FA Cup they had to be grateful for a late equaliser by Gordon Harris at home to Leyton Orient. As if stung by criticism of their performance, Burnley took their frustration out on Birmingham, thrashing them 7-1 at Turf Moor. They made harder work of Orient in the cup replay, hanging on to win 1-0 thanks to a Brian Miller goal. Burnley were drawn at home to Everton in the last 16.

Miller was instrumental in their 3-1 FA Cup victory against Everton, a talented and emerging team that would win the championship in 1963. The Merseysiders led at half-time, but within a minute of the restart Miller had levelled. John Connelly and Jimmy Robson added further goals and Burnley were through. *The Times* was quick to trumpet their achievement, 'Burnley, its industrial face grey in shade, is set in a hollow ringed by cold moors where even the sheep look drab. But as leaders of the league and now once again in the last eight of the FA Cup, its football shines on a pinnacle.'

Such praise seemed to amplify by the week as Burnley homed in on the season's climax. After beating contenders West Ham United 6-0 at the start of March, pundits predicted the club could start planning for the European Cup in 1962/63 and that barring a seismic event, they would be champions for the second time in three years. It helped that Tottenham, who were now eyeing European success, had imploded at Manchester City and were beaten 6-2. Ipswich, though, were keeping pace and had overtaken Spurs.

Burnley's resilience in the FA Cup came to the fore again in the sixth round at Bramall Lane, Sheffield United's three-sided ground. The Blades won the tie on points, but in terms of goals, Burnley's 52nd-minute strike from Ray Pointer was enough to see them into the semi-finals.

Burnley were now a handful of games away from spectacular success, although the size of their squad was relatively small and the players were tiring. While they were drawing at Cardiff, Ipswich were almost ending Tottenham's title bid, winning 3-1 at White Hart Lane. On the same evening, Fulham secured their place in the last four of the FA Cup and would meet Burnley. Tottenham and Manchester United were the other semi-finalists. The league table demonstrated it was now a two-horse race with Burnley top on 43 points and Ipswich a point behind after playing two more games.

Burnley had started to lose a little belief and their lead was being eroded. Their clash with Spurs more or less finished the champions' hopes but a 2-2 draw could have been more damaging – if Ipswich had beaten Blackpool they would have drawn level with Burnley on points. The FA Cup got in the way a little for while Burnley were preparing and then playing Fulham in the semi, Ipswich won two more games and took top spot with 48 points from 36 games. Burnley had no fewer than four matches in hand, but they were also a little jaded. A draw with Fulham at Villa Park did not help the cause.

Ipswich were doing their best to keep the contest open and were soundly beaten 5-0 at Manchester United on 7 April, a result that would have been even more humiliating if goalkeeper Roy Bailey had not been on his best form. Burnley went top again after a 1-1 stalemate with Wolves and they were favourites for the league as they had three games more to play. Just 48 hours later, they clinched their place in the FA Cup Final by beating Fulham 2-0 in their semi-final replay in Nottingham. So now Harry Potts knew what he had to do to take more silverware to Turf Moor – beat their old rivals Tottenham at Wembley. They could concentrate on the league until 5 May, but they had eight games to play between 11 and 30 April.

Burnley drew 0-0 at Bolton in the first of those eight fixtures which gave them a one-point advantage over Ipswich, but disaster struck twice in a four-day period for the league leaders. Manchester United, who were no more than a mid-table side, won 3-1 at Turf Moor against a Burnley team that lacked Jimmy McIlroy, Jimmy Adamson and Brian Miller.

While Potts's men slipped up, Ipswich scraped home 1-0 against Cardiff and went back into pole position.

Worse was to come for Burnley as they lost at home to Blackburn Rovers by a solitary first-half goal. Burnley pounded the visitors' goal in the second half and Pointer almost levelled in the dying embers of the game, but another defeat meant they had gone five games without a win and they were one point behind Ipswich with just one game in hand.

Burnley bounced back with a 2-0 victory against Blackpool at home, but then lost at Sheffield United. Ipswich, however, picked up two points in drawn games with Arsenal and Chelsea, both of which were earned after falling two goals behind. Burnley were struggling, however, and could only draw at Blackpool while Ipswich won impressively at Arsenal. Alf Ramsey's underrated side, described as a team of cast-offs that did things simply, quickly and accurately, were now two points in front of Burnley although the Clarets had two games to play versus Ipswich's one. Burnley also had a better goal average, so the title-winning ribbons could still be in their colours.

Alas, it was all over on 28 April as Burnley were held 1-1 at home by already relegated Chelsea. Ipswich ploughed on, scoring two late goals to beat Aston Villa at Portman Road. They had a three-point margin and could not be caught. Burnley still had the FA Cup to come and there was some consolation in Jimmy Adamson being named Footballer of the Year, but they knew they had thrown away the league title. Ipswich, on the other hand, had been relentless and totally efficient. Their success would become a footballing fairy tale.

The FA Cup Final was billed as the 'final of the century' as it involved two of the best footballing teams in England. The hacks tipped Spurs to win; they had finished the season with only one defeat in 11 games while Burnley had won two in 12. Burnley seemed exhausted and had seen their confidence and form suffer. Spurs also knew Wembley and its rich turf after winning the FA Cup the previous year. They had Jimmy Greaves in their ranks and his presence had added a certain sophistication to the way they played. Furthermore, Spurs had benefitted from their European Cup experience and had gone so close to reaching the final, denied by Portugal's Benfica.

The tipsters were correct in their assumption. Both teams played superbly and with joyful enthusiasm. Greaves scored after three minutes, displaying speed and rapier-like finishing, and the match remained 1-0 into the second half. Burnley levelled five minutes after the restart through Jimmy Robson, but almost immediately, Bobby Smith restored Spurs' lead. Lord, recalling the way the holders responded, said, 'I thought we were getting on top but they hit back like that.' Potts was insistent that Smith had fouled Brian Miller before scoring, although the recording of the game didn't support his view. It remained that way until nine minutes from the end when Tommy Cummings handled the ball in the area and Danny Blanchflower scored Spurs' third goal from the penalty spot. The cup went back to White Hart Lane.

There was plenty of sympathy for Burnley, who had been outstanding for months, but really had run out of steam. The final had lived up to expectations but Spurs deserved their triumph. Burnley were, without doubt, the unluckiest of nearly men. They went close again in 1962/63, finishing third in the league, but fans' favourite Jimmy McIlroy, who was 31 years old, was sold to Stoke City for £25,000, prompting the Burnley faithful to claim chairman Lord was insane. They also blamed Potts who had apparently told McIlroy his performances hadn't been good enough.

Burnley continued to develop talent throughout the 1960s and into the 1970s, including numerous players – Ralph Coates, David Thomas, Martin Dobson and others – who were eventually sold for big money. But Burnley's momentum started to fade and they slipped into mid-table and then the relegation zone. The period between 1959 and 1962 was a golden time for the club and although they remain overachievers today, to quote Harold Macmillan, the UK prime minister of the late 1950s, Burnley had 'never had it so good'.

9

Chelsea 1965: Docherty's flawed diamonds

MODERN CHELSEA have had no shortage of triumphant processions, but until they were taken over by Roman Abramovich in 2003 success had often eluded London's most enigmatic club. Indeed, up until 1997, Chelsea had won a single league title, one FA Cup, a solitary League Cup and one European Cup Winners' Cup. For 94 years they were one of the game's great underachievers. They were also a self-destructive club, often the cause of their own downfall. There's no telling how much more success they might have had were it not for their habit of rocking the boat when stability was needed. They have often lacked the influence of a cool head in the heat of battle.

In 1961/62, Chelsea were relegated from the First Division just seven years after winning at that time their only league championship in 1955. They had disposed of the man who led them to that triumph, Ted Drake, and appointed coach Tommy Docherty as manager. The team that had pulled off that unlikely victory had long since dispersed; it was a relatively mature side so winning the league had taken a lot out of them. As they drifted away, Chelsea saw their future depending on the development of players in their youth scheme. In 1960 and 1961, Chelsea's youngsters won the FA Youth Cup. The club wanted to emulate what Matt Busby had achieved at Manchester United in the form of his 'Busby Babes', many of whom had perished in the snow at Munich airport in February 1958.

Docherty hoped to harness the potential at his disposal at Chelsea to build a young, vibrant team that would excite the London public. Fitness, intense discipline and innovation were high on the agenda. With his short-cropped hair, parade ground manner and caustic Glaswegian sense of humour, there was something vaguely militaristic about Docherty.

Relegation in 1962 was a bitter blow, but Docherty pledged to build his new Chelsea around homegrown talent. In 1962/63 they looked promotion material from the off, although a prolonged winter and a stuttering run-in meant they were struggling to stay in the top two places in the Second Division. Ironically, it was an old hand who set up promotion in the form of ex-Tottenham favourite Tommy Harmer. His unorthodox goal, turned in off his jockstrap, won Chelsea a vital clash at Sunderland in the penultimate fixture. Chelsea had to face Portsmouth in the final game and won 7-0 to clinch promotion.

Docherty felt he had a team good enough to do more than merely survive in the top flight. As he celebrated Chelsea's triumph against Pompey, he cupped his hands and shouted to the crowd from the directors' box, 'Now we will give you a team to be proud of for many years to come.'

In 1963/64 Chelsea surprised a few people and finished fifth in the First Division. The essence of energetic youth was found in players such as Peter Bonetti, Ken Shellito, Ron Harris, Terry Venables, Bobby Tambling and Bert Murray forming the backbone of the team – all of whom came from the colts. Tambling, who captained Chelsea to promotion, was just 21 and had already been capped twice by England. He was seen as one of English football's rising stars after emerging from of the shadow of Jimmy Greaves, who had left Chelsea in 1961 for AC Milan.

Docherty strengthened his squad in early season by signing central defender Marvin Hinton from Charlton Athletic for £35,000, but apart from young squad members he relied on the players he felt could improve and take Chelsea to a new level. Derek Kevan, who was supposed to add experience to the side, had been disappointing and the club cut its losses and sold him to Manchester City. So committed to this approach were Chelsea that they disposed of their chief scout, Jimmy Thompson.

After beating Tottenham in the FA Cup, Chelsea surprisingly lost at home to Huddersfield in the next round, but their run-in to the end of the campaign saw them lose just once in nine games and secure fifth place. They actually finished their 42 league games in third, but both Everton and Spurs overtook them when they caught up on their fixtures. It had been their best season since the title win.

The manner in which Chelsea had grown comfortable in the First Division led some pundits to predict a fine season in 1964/65. While admitting that the main power in English football lay in the north – Liverpool, Everton and Manchester United – Chelsea were among the teams that could be surprise contenders, 'If they do not allow their legs to run away with their wits.' Chelsea were seen as a whirling dervish of a team, capable of playing fast, attacking football, but lacking some composure and maturity. They were the youngest team in the division, with an average age of under 24 years.

Chelsea's vigour was matched by a newly promoted Leeds United team managed by Don Revie. There were certain similarities between the two line-ups and as a result, as two members outside of the establishment, they had their own rivalry to contend with. Leeds also had young players who had been nurtured by Revie and his backroom staff. The Yorkshire club, who had gained a reputation for uncompromising tactics, were a surprise package in 1964/65 and they quickly became title contenders. When Chelsea hosted them in September, a match won 2-0 by Docherty's team, the media claimed it had been 'a foul a minute' and 'a brute of a game'.

By this time Chelsea had demonstrated their credentials and were top of the table with points to spare. The season had been just four minutes old when they took the lead at Wolverhampton Wanderers through Tambling, displaying their speed and breathless style. 'Chelsea jet boys', 'space-age soccer' and 'whizz kids' were the type of references made to a dynamic style of football that made even the most celebrated players look leaden-footed. Others were less impressed, complaining that Chelsea were monotonous and formulaic.

Chelsea won their first three games, beating Aston Villa and Sunderland after the opener at Wolves. George Graham, a 19-year-old forward signed from Villa, made his debut against Sunderland and scored as his new club won 3-1. Three draws followed, against Villa, Leicester and Sheffield Wednesday, before Chelsea won five consecutive games, taking them three points clear of second-placed Blackpool. They were unbeaten in their first ten matches but there was a shock or two ahead of Docherty and his bright side.

Manchester United, complete with the holy trinity of Bobby Charlton, Denis Law and the up-and-coming George Best, arrived at Stamford Bridge after trouncing Tottenham 4-1 at Old Trafford. This was arguably the match of the league season so far and over 60,000 packed into the stadium to see two of the country's best teams. Chelsea's line-up had cost just ten per cent of United's outlay of £300,000.

This was a real test for Chelsea and they failed, losing 2-0 with United scoring a goal in each half through Best and

Law. The two sides were well-matched, possessing a similar sense of urgency about them. Where United differentiated themselves was in individual skill and flair, but with the likes of Law and Best in their line-up it was hardly surprising. Best, in particular, had the crowd purring with delight every time he received the ball. He gave Ken Shellito a torrid time on the flank and received an ovation from the home fans.

For the first time, Chelsea realised that there were teams who would not roll over as victims of their high-octane onslaughts. They were still top, but United were menacing and just two points behind. Chelsea responded well, emphatically beating Blackburn (5-1) and Stoke City (4-0) at home and grabbing draws at Nottingham Forest and Tottenham. While they were battling away at White Hart Lane, United thrashed Aston Villa 7-0 with Law scoring four times. The lead had been cut to one point.

One month after United had won at Stamford Bridge, a young Burnley team lowered Chelsea's colours at home again, securing a 1-0 victory in an ill-tempered match in which the Londoners appeared to lose their nerve. For a couple of weeks the chief orchestrator of the team, Terry Venables, had appeared off colour and against Burnley, he was so off form that the shape and function of the team went astray. *The Times* noted, 'It is an inherent weakness of Chelsea's machine-like style that they rely so heavily on Venables.' The defeat could not have come at a worse time as Manchester United pulled off a 2-0 win at Liverpool and went to the top. Chelsea, for the first time in a while, were not the leaders.

Once more they responded well, winning three games and scoring 13 goals with Graham netting five of them, including a 5-1 victory over 1963 league champions Everton. But it was clear all was not well in the Chelsea side when they were beaten 3-0 at home by West Ham, who played intelligent and progressive football under Ron Greenwood, a former Chelsea player. It was getting very competitive, with Manchester United now three points clear and Leeds one point behind.

There were distractions from the league programme, however, and Chelsea had worked their way through to the last four of the League Cup. They beat Workington in the quarter-finals after a replay that was won 2-0 at an empty Stamford Bridge. A gangly 17-year-old called Peter Osgood was blooded by Docherty and he obliged by scoring two goals in the last ten minutes. The fans caught no further sight of the promising forward in 1964/65, but they would not have to wait too long to discover a new hero. Docherty was so excited by Osgood that he compared him to England frontmen Johnny Byrne and the late Tommy Taylor.

Chelsea ended 1964 one point behind Manchester United, but it was now very much a three-horse race for the title as Leeds had also been in consistent form. There was a blow to Chelsea's hopes when coach Dave Sexton was hired by Orient to be their manager. Some said his departure meant Docherty's more explosive nature was more exposed, and now he didn't have the calming influence of jazz enthusiast Sexton.

The FA Cup third round arrived and Chelsea easily disposed of Northampton before meeting West Ham at Upton Park on the day of Sir Winston Churchill's funeral. They won 1-0 to set up a fifth-round tie with Tottenham at home.

Chelsea managed to keep former hero Jimmy Greaves quiet and won 1-0 thanks to a goal from Barry Bridges. Docherty wasn't pleased with the performance, but the bookmakers were confident they would end up with some serious silverware and made them 9-1 favourites to win the double.

The League Cup semi-final saw Chelsea beat Aston Villa 4-3 on aggregate, earned by a 3-2 victory at Villa Park thanks to a winning goal from debutant John Boyle, and a 1-1 draw at Stamford Bridge. Their opponents in the final would be Leicester City, the holders.

There was a setback in the league with a 1-0 home defeat at the hands of Nottingham Forest, whose goal came from a John Barnwell volley. Chelsea hammered away at the Forest defence in the second half but there could be no denying that it was not good for their title hopes, even though they were still top with 44 points, the same tally as Leeds and three ahead of Manchester United.

Fixtures were coming thick and fast, though, and Chelsea were feeling the strain. Peterborough were beaten in the FA Cup sixth round and then Spurs lost 3-1 at Stamford Bridge, giving Chelsea a three-point margin over Leeds and five over Manchester United. It was one of the best performances in weeks and rekindled hopes the title could be won. The next game, at Old Trafford, would go a long way to determining the destination of the ornate trophy.

The match was a disaster for Chelsea, who were torn apart by the wayward genius of Best once more. United scored two goals in each half and could have had more. But the visitors won praise for the way they accepted defeat, even though they were taunted by the United fans singing, 'Goodbye, Chelsea, we'll see you again.' The vanquished, meanwhile, applauded the home team off the pitch after a 4-0 humbling.

Amazingly Chelsea were still top, although they had played one game more than both Leeds and United. If Docherty was crestfallen, he didn't let it show, 'You wait, on the day they were the better side, but we'll still be there at the finish.' Chelsea's methodical and, some might say, dogmatic style, as opposed to United's improvisational 'off-the-cuff' approach, was simply brushed aside.

Two days later, Chelsea beat Leicester in the first leg of the League Cup Final. A poorly attended occasion, with just 20,000 in the vast, rainswept Stamford Bridge, saw Eddie McCreadie (who had experienced a torrid time at Old Trafford thanks to Best) score the clincher as Chelsea won 3-2. Only an outstanding performance from Leicester's England goalkeeper, Gordon Banks, prevented the holders from a bigger defeat.

The Manchester United reverse could have knocked a young side's confidence, but a 3-0 win against Sheffield United kept them top on goal average over Leeds and one better than the Red Devils, who had now played a game more. Chelsea's next match was the FA Cup semi-final against Liverpool at Villa Park.

The FA Cup's last four could hardly have been stronger, comprising the top three of the First Division plus reigning league champions Liverpool. While Chelsea and Liverpool were battling it out in Birmingham, Leeds and Manchester United met at Hillsborough. The press enjoyed the thought of a Chelsea–United final but they didn't get their wish.

Chelsea were mild favourites, even though Liverpool were the league champions and had won through to the last four of the European Cup. They were confident and even went as far as producing a cup final brochure in advance, which was, apparently, the work of their skipper Terry Venables. Bill Shankly managed to get a copy and used it as a motivational tool for his players.

Chelsea thought they had scored after 22 minutes when John Mortimore headed home a Tambling corner. The referee ruled it out and Chelsea were never quite the same. It was still goalless at half-time, but in the 62nd minute Peter Thompson swept a brilliant left-footed drive past Bonetti. 'Once they scored, there was only one side in it,' recalled Docherty. Thompson, a mainstay in the Liverpool team in the 1960s, was outstanding and enjoyed the freedom the Chelsea defence gave him.

With 12 minutes remaining Ron Harris upended Ian St John, and Willie Stevenson drove home from the penalty spot. Liverpool were at Wembley and Chelsea trooped off, stunned that they had not reached their first FA Cup Final since 1915. They had not performed when it really mattered, a fact that did not go unnoticed. 'How was it that this team of virile youngsters, often criticised for running too much, suddenly became like old men whose legs would not carry them where they wanted to go?' said one scribe.

The occasion had been too much for a young side, but Liverpool, for all their experience, were only marginally older than the Chelsea line-up. Shankly's team had, however, cost three times as much (£132,500 versus £40,000). Although the First Division's youngest team had shown its lack of savvy, there were encouraging words from *The Times*, which said of Chelsea, 'Their sap is still rising: there will be another spring.'

The current spring was proving to be taxing, though. A draw at Everton was followed by a win against Birmingham. Chelsea were top with six games to go, one point clear of Leeds, who had a game in hand, and two in front of Manchester United. The League Cup was won after a 0-0 draw in the second leg of the final at Leicester, so Chelsea had some silverware, albeit a relatively minor trophy at that time.

At West Ham on 12 April, the title race began to unfold. Chelsea were 3-0 down in 25 minutes and showed great character in staging a comeback but eventually lost 3-2. Leeds came from behind to win 2-1 at West Bromwich and Manchester United beat a stubborn Leicester 1-0. Chelsea had slipped to third, level on points with United but three behind Leeds. All three contenders had played 37 games and Leeds appeared to have the easier task in their final five. The first of those, however, was at home to Manchester United.

Leeds had not been beaten for 25 games but an early goal from John Connelly gave United a 1-0 win. Chelsea slipped up against West Bromwich Albion, drawing 2-2 at Stamford Bridge in front of a disgruntled home crowd. Chelsea were now back on top – they had thrashed Liverpool a couple of days earlier – but now the other two challengers were in a better position. On Easter Monday, Liverpool repeated their FA Cup success with a 2-0 victory at Anfield, prompting the Kop to sing, 'Ee-aye-adio, Chelsea have lost the league.'

If that was the case, then Leeds had also stumbled after a 3-0 defeat at Hillsborough in the Yorkshire derby with Sheffield Wednesday. Manchester United, meanwhile, won 4-2 at Birmingham, relegating the home side and sending themselves back to the top. They were only one point ahead of Chelsea and Leeds, but they had played a game fewer than the Londoners.

It did look as though Chelsea had run out of ideas, but they had two relatively comfortable games left, at Burnley and Blackpool. Leeds went back to the top after beating Wednesday 2-0, but Manchester United were the favourites now. Chelsea were almost done.

Chelsea travelled to Lancashire and decided to stay in Blackpool over the weekend rather than make two journeys. Their last roll of the dice was really the game at Burnley's Turf Moor. They needed to win just to keep their interest alive. On the Friday, at around 3am, Tommy Docherty heard a commotion in their hotel and discovered that the bulk of his team had been out until 1am, apparently at a bowling alley.

Docherty, clearly frustrated by his team's capitulation in the title race, went berserk and sent eight players back to London – Venables, Bridges, Murray, Graham, Fascione, Hollins, Hinton and McCreadie. 'I feel this was the only way to do it. The club is more important than any individual player or the league championship. How can you win the championship with disloyal players?' he said.

What followed was pure theatre and suggested Docherty had milked the situation by informing the press that the heart of his team was being sent home in disgrace. When the players arrived in London they were surrounded by cameras, policemen and other interested parties. The photographs in the newspapers made the players appear like criminals being escorted from Euston station by uniformed officers. Would Docherty have acted in the way he did if Chelsea's title hopes were still intact? It is doubtful.

Docherty may have been influenced by the approach taken by Inter Milan's Argentinian coach Helenio Herrera, the ultra-disciplinarian who presided over a cynical and ruthless team that won the European Cup in 1965. 'The Chelsea boys were lucky this was England and not, say, Italy, Yugoslavia or Peru,' said the *Daily Mirror*'s Sam Leitch, who described Herrera as the 'black-haired dictator of European football'.

Docherty drafted in seven new players, including two debutants and, unsurprisingly, Chelsea were thrashed at Burnley, who went a goal ahead within a minute and by half-time led 4-1. Andy Lochhead, Burnley's centre-forward, scored five as they ran out 6-2 winners. The title dream was over; it was now Leeds or Manchester United for the big prize.

Although Chelsea chairman Joe Mears backed Docherty to the hilt, six players were restored to the team for the final game at Blackpool, which was also lost. Manchester United clinched the title on 26 April on goal average, beating Arsenal 3-1 while Leeds were held 3-3 at Birmingham.

Docherty was philosophical, even though some people felt he had gone too far. Popular myth says Chelsea's trip to Lancashire cost them the title, but even two victories would not have been enough. 'We want to prove next season that we have a great side,' he said.

Third in the league, qualification for Europe, the League Cup in the trophy cabinet and the FA Cup semi-finals – an excellent season in so many ways, but there was the underlying feeling that Chelsea could so easily have been champions. Their relatively small squad, a lack of experience and a style of play that may have been slightly inflexible was their undoing.

In 1965/66 they enjoyed another good campaign, although they were never in contention for the league. Again they fell at the semi-final stages, in both the FA Cup and Inter-Cities Fairs Cup. Docherty lost patience with some of his players, notably Venables, who didn't have the best relationship with the manager after the Blackpool incident, and so he sold him to Tottenham. In 1966/67 Chelsea finally reached Wembley, but lost to Tottenham, and Venables, in the FA Cup Final.

Chelsea remained, to a certain degree, underachievers for the next few decades, but the team that went so close to gaining legendary status among their fans has never been forgotten, even as they count their trophies in the 21st century.

10

Rangers 1968: In any other year

THINK OF Scottish football in the 1960s and early 1970s and you immediately think of Celtic, Jock Stein, the Lisbon Lions and Jimmy Johnstone. Yet people often forget that Celtic didn't have absolutely everything their own way and they were often made to fight hard for their silverware. A fine team, for sure, but during that time, Celtic's bitter rivals Rangers also had some excellent players.

Between 1965/66 and 1973/74, Celtic won 19 out of a possible 27 Scottish honours. Rangers won just three in that time frame and were runners-up in the league on six occasions. The average deficit in those six campaigns was 4.1 points, hardly a story of a runaway train for the green side of Glasgow, but enough to see off all genuine challengers.

The Old Firm dominated Scottish football and their attendances told the full story – both teams averaged over 30,000 in 1967, the year of Celtic's historic quadruple success. Nobody else could match those figures. The national team also reflected the influence of Celtic and Rangers, with as many as eight players drawn from both clubs representing Scotland in 1967/68.

Rangers were completely overshadowed by Celtic in 1966/67 and when they lost to Berwick Rangers in the Scottish

Cup, it was seen as a sign that an overhaul was needed at Ibrox Park. 'Wee Berwick KO cup-holders Rangers' was a headline that haunted the Gers for years.

Furthermore, they no longer had their talismanic but erratic midfielder, Jim Baxter, who had been sold to Sunderland for £70,000 in the summer of 1965. Baxter still had enough lustre to star in Scotland's legendary 3-2 win at Wembley as they became the first team to beat England after their 1966 World Cup triumph.

In the close season of 1967, Rangers hired the up-and-coming David White from Clyde as long-serving manager Scot Symon's assistant. In truth, it looked as though Rangers wanted a younger man to mould the team and provide a more contemporary opponent to Celtic. Rangers spent liberally to build their challenge. Almost £200,000 was splashed out on players including Alec Smith of Dunfermline, Dave Smith of Aberdeen, Dundee's Andy Penman and Swedish winger Örjan Persson.

While Celtic won everything in 1967, Rangers were hardly no-hopers. They had finished runners-up in the league by just three points and reached the European Cup Winners' Cup Final, narrowly losing to the rising Bayern Munich in extra time in Nuremberg just six days after Celtic had won the European Cup in Lisbon. If Rangers had pulled off a victory in Germany, it would have completed a remarkable double for Glasgow and Scotland.

Bayern Munich had Franz Beckenbauer and Gerd Müller in their ranks, two players who would become household names in the years that followed. Rangers played well, their defence was strong and withstood most of the Bayern attacks, but up front the Scots could not penetrate a strong back line. 'Every Ranger played his heart out,' said Symon. The extra-time winner came from Franz Roth, a player who had a knack of scoring vital goals in finals. Some pundits felt Rangers didn't deserve to lose, but Bayern went on to make a career out of strategically managing big games and wearing their opponents down. Bayern's coach Zlatko Čajkovski, generous in victory, said Rangers were 'world-class'.

Rangers had gone close to having a standout season, but Celtic's achievements meant they were dissatisfied and desperate to bounce back in 1967/68.

Among the new faces arriving at the club was one Alex Ferguson of Dunfermline, the man who would become one of the greatest managers of all time with Manchester United. Danish goalkeeper Erik Sørensen also joined from Morton as well as defender Alex Miller, who enjoyed a long career with the Gers.

Rangers kicked off the 1967/68 season in fine style, winning 2-0 at Partick Thistle with both goals scored by Andy Penman. Then came the Old Firm derby with Celtic, and despite losing David Provan to a broken leg they won 1-0 at Ibrox Park, with Persson scoring after beating three defenders and shooting low past Ronnie Simpson. It was Celtic's first defeat since their European triumph, so local bragging rights were intense and prolonged. In their first ten games, Rangers conceded just four goals and kept seven clean sheets.

At the end of October Rangers were top of the table, unbeaten in their first eight, and although they had been held at home to a 0-0 draw by Dunfermline, a game that saw the team jeered off the pitch, they were in reasonably good shape. Then, on 1 November, rumours started circulating Glasgow that Symon had been sacked despite their impressive start to the season. Symon had, apparently, been advised by the club's accountant that he had been released from his role and David White had been installed in his place. Rangers, apparently, had not officially advised Symon he was no longer in charge.

There was no small amount of confusion about the incident and to this day, people believe Symon was let go because

Rangers were simply becoming very nervous about Celtic and Jock Stein. There was no doubt Symon was 'old-school', but the modern manager in 1967 had to have a sound business head as well as coaching capabilities. Stein certainly had those qualities in abundance.

Some felt Symon, who had been with Rangers for 13 years and presided over a successful era, had been treated badly and used as a scapegoat for the dominance of Celtic. Stein, who was in South America with his team for the World Club Championship game with Racing Club, sent a message of support to his rival and hoped to catch up with him upon his return. Two days after Symon's supposed sacking, coach Bobby Seith resigned in protest about the treatment of the manager. 'I no longer wish to be part of an organisation which can treat a loyal servant so badly,' he said.

Rangers were, after all, leading the table, but the club's directors said there had been a lack of goals given the investment made in new forwards. Cynics believed it was as much a response to public unrest as anything else. It took a fortnight, but Rangers and Symon settled the issue amicably and the man who led them to six league titles was made an honorary member of the club.

White began his new job with an away game at St Johnstone, a 3-2 win that triggered a flurry of goalscoring, the very thing the club's suited management were calling for in the latter days of Symon. Rangers won nine games in a row, including a 10-2 victory at Raith Rovers. As 1967 ended, White's side won 4-1 at Aberdeen to maintain a two-point lead over Celtic. Rangers were still unbeaten, while Celtic's loss at Ibrox in September was still their only one in the league. Celtic's defence of the European Cup ended prematurely and surprisingly in the first round against Dynamo Kiev in September.

On 2 January, the Old Firm met at Parkhead in their traditional holiday clash with 73,000 people in attendance.

Celtic took an early lead through Bertie Auld, but Willie Johnston levelled ten minutes into the second half. With 12 minutes to go Bobby Murdoch made it 2-1, but with time running out, Celtic's stand-in keeper John Fallon slipped up and allowed Kai Johansen to equalise. It was Fallon's second blunder of the game. The 2-2 draw was seen as something of a title indicator if not decider, even though there were still 16 matches to go. The action might have been frenetic, but off the field the scorecard of four arrests and five taken to hospital was considered to have been a quiet, low-key afternoon.

Rangers followed the big Glasgow clash with a comfortable win against Falkirk before travelling to Edinburgh to face Hearts. Before the game, Rangers complained about the state of pitches in Scotland, which in January became hazardous and made good football impossible. At Tynecastle, they skated to a 3-2 win.

Rangers won their next eight in a row, scoring an average of three goals per game. At the beginning of March they beat St Johnstone 6-2 with Alex Ferguson scoring four times. On the same day, though, Celtic won 6-0 at Kilmarnock. Rangers were now four points ahead of their neighbours, who had had a game in hand. Celtic were in top form, however, and were winning as relentlessly as Rangers.

Celtic were proud of the fact their glorious 1967 team was drawn almost from the neighbourhood. Rangers may not have built their own side from Glasgow youngsters, but like Celtic, they had a cluster of players who had graduated through their youth and reserve teams. They were now quite experienced performers, though. John Greig, David Provan, Willie Henderson and Ronnie McKinnon (along with Jim Baxter) had all played in the club's treble-winning team of 1963/64.

Greig, the club's captain, was an outstanding player who was widely recognised for his leadership qualities. But he was not a native of Glasgow; Greig was from Edinburgh and a Hearts supporter as a boy. He also captained Scotland and won a total of 44 caps for his country, just missing out on the 1974 World Cup. Greig was ranked as the 'greatest Ranger' in a poll conducted by the club. He started out as a forward but moved to midfield and finally, left-back. Not for nothing is there a statue of Greig at Ibrox Park.

McKinnon formed, with Greig and Baxter, a legendary half-back line for Rangers in the early 1960s. A powerful central defender, he was cool, composed and intelligent on the ball, possessing strong aerial ability. He was also fast, claiming to be the swiftest player at the club even when he was over 30. There was always an ongoing debate in Glasgow as to who was the best centre-half, McKinnon or Celtic's Billy McNeill. McKinnon was also a suave character who was particular about his appearance, which must have earned him some ribbing from his team-mates.

Provan was another homegrown player and his time with the club dated back to 1958 when he made his league debut. Born in Falkirk, Provan won five caps for Scotland and stayed at Ibrox until 1970 when he moved south to join Crystal Palace.

Henderson was another product of the Rangers system, a tricky and industrious player whose eyesight was not as good as his wing play. Henderson was short-sighted and often had difficulties, but he was still able to win 29 caps for Scotland and enjoy a 20-year career. Henderson's rival for a place in the national team was none other than Jimmy Johnstone of Celtic. Like Johnstone, he was only 5ft 4in tall, so inevitably, he was known as 'Wee Willie'. Henderson had to endure some injuries in 1967/68, notably a fractured jaw and a problem with a cartilage in his knee.

Sandy Jardine was just 19 in 1967/68 and was one of the younger players introduced after the cup defeat by Berwick Rangers in 1967. He played in the European Cup Winners'

Cup Final that year and a handful of league games in the following season. He went on to win 38 caps for Scotland and played in two World Cups, in 1974 and 1978. He stayed with Rangers until 1982, when he joined Hearts, the club of his formative years.

Willie Johnston left school and became a miner before joining Rangers. He made his debut as a 17-year-old and became a close friend of Baxter in his early years at the club. Johnston had two spells with Rangers but the success of Celtic meant he won few medals. He did earn 22 caps for Scotland, playing briefly in the 1978 World Cup as a 31-year-old. Sadly, he was sent home from Argentina after failing a drug test owing to the use of medication to treat hay fever.

Rangers also had two Danes in their squad in Kai Johansen and Erik Sørensen. Both arrived via Greenock Morton, who had brought to Scotland a cluster of Scandinavians, including Preben Arentoft and Per Bartram, who went on to play in England for Newcastle United and Crystal Palace respectively.

Both Johansen and Sørensen were from Odense, a city better known as the birthplace of Hans Christian Andersen. Johansen joined Rangers in 1965, costing his new club £20,000. A full-back, he guaranteed his place in Rangers folklore when he scored the winning goal in the 1966 Scottish Cup Final against Celtic. Goalkeeper Sørensen arrived from Morton in 1967 but only stayed for a short while before returning to Greenock.

While the league form was excellent, Rangers suffered some disappointing blows in cup competitions. Firstly, in the quarter-finals of the Scottish Cup, Hearts beat them 1-0 in a replay at Tynecastle, Donald Ford scoring two minutes from the end. The game was marred by pitch invasions – there were 44,000 in the ground – and 40 people were injured due to overcrowding. Defeat for Rangers and Celtic earlier in the competition meant the semi-finals did not include either of the Old Firm giants for only the third time in 21 years.

Rangers also fell short in the Inter-Cities Fairs Cup, a competition that was growing in stature after a staccato beginning. Rangers had beaten Dynamo Dresden, dramatically with a Greig goal in the final minute just seconds after the East Germans had levelled, and narrowly disposed of Köln 4-3 on aggregate. Their opponents in the last eight were Leeds United, who had already beaten Scotland's Hibernian in the competition.

Leeds were a team in the ascendancy, chasing every trophy they could lay their hands on. They had already won their first major piece of silverware in 1967/68, lifting the League Cup at the beginning of March 1968 after beating Arsenal at Wembley in a bad-tempered contest. At the time they were a raw outfit, specialists in 'cold-eyed professionalism' and a little over-zealous with their tackling and challenges. A crowd of 79,000 packed Ibrox for what was billed as 'the Battle of Britain' just as Leeds' clash with Celtic in 1970 was. Leeds were top of the Football League and Rangers were second in Scotland, but favourites to win the league. It was a tough evening, played in wind and driving rain, but Leeds' defensive screen held firm. The game ended goalless and most people wrote off Rangers' chances for the second leg.

Predictably, Leeds won the second leg to claim their place in the semi-finals. Two first-half goals, a penalty from Johnny Giles and one from Peter Lorimer, gave Don Revie's team a 2-0 victory. There was crowd trouble, sadly, as bottles were thrown on to the pitch. Some 20,000 Rangers fans had travelled down to Yorkshire, turning Leeds into a suburb of Glasgow.

With no further interest in cup competitions for either Rangers or Celtic, the remainder of the season was a case of two heavyweights slugging it out for the title. On 2 April, Rangers spurned the chance to steal a march on their rivals when they met Dundee United at Tannadice. They drew 0-0 on a desperate evening but went a point clear of Celtic. They had both played 29 games.

Both contenders won on the first weekend of April and Celtic followed that up with a 1-0 victory against Aberdeen, consequently taking over the leadership. On 13 April, Rangers threw away a two-goal half-time lead at Raith, eventually winning 3-2 thanks to a Penman strike, while Celtic notched up their 100th league goal of the season as they beat Dundee 5-2 at Parkhead. Celtic were a point ahead but Rangers had a game more to play. Four days later, they made the short trip to Morton, knowing a win would tip the needle in their direction once more.

But the game was a disaster for Rangers and their title hopes as Morton took a 2-0 lead in the first half through Tony Taylor and Joe Mason. Greig tried to inspire Rangers and pulled a goal back just after the interval. Morton came straight back and restored their two-goal advantage in the 49th minute. Again, Rangers tried to respond but it took another Greig goal 20 minutes from time to reduce the arrears. In the 80th minute Willie Johnston headed the equaliser to save a point, but the result had tipped the scales with both teams now on 59 points but Celtic had a vastly superior goal average. The task for Rangers was clear – they had to outperform Celtic in results over the last two games. The smart money was now being placed on the Bhoys.

For their penultimate games, both showed signs of nerves. At Parkhead, the Celtic fans welcomed Morton on to the pitch with grateful applause after their draw with Rangers. Celtic then bombarded Morton's defence for most of the 90 minutes, but had to rely on a Bobby Lennox goal right at the end to win 2-1. At Kilmarnock's Rugby Park, a battered and bruised Rangers went a goal down but came back to equalise through Persson. The Swedish winger's replacement Alex Willoughby, a player who had been out of favour earlier in the season, netted the winner to ease the tension for Rangers. At one stage, news had arrived from Glasgow that Celtic had drawn, prompting a minor pitch invasion from Rangers fans celebrating another twist in the championship race.

Both teams had one game to play and were level on points, but Celtic's final fixture, at Dunfermline, was rescheduled to 30 April as their opponents were playing in the Scottish Cup Final at Hampden on 27 April. Rangers were at home to Aberdeen on the same day, but this clearly put the Gers at something of a disadvantage as Celtic would know exactly what they had to do in their final game. Rangers had to win on cup final day to complete their fixtures and then hope that Celtic slipped up. This scenario would not be permitted in the modern game with both teams playing on the same day.

While Dunfermline were winning the Scottish Cup against Hearts, Rangers were slipping up at Ibrox. Nobody gave Aberdeen much hope of winning in Glasgow but they did, 3-2, and in doing so they secured a place in Europe for 1968/69.

Dave Smith gave Rangers the lead after 17 minutes, but Davie Johnston equalised for Aberdeen before half-time. Alex Ferguson headed Rangers' second goal but Johnston netted again for the Dons. Even a draw was not good news for Rangers, but they couldn't even get that as Ian Taylor scored a third for the visitors in the final minute. Aberdeen won 3-2 to send Rangers to their first and only defeat of the league campaign, and at the same time, give the title to Celtic, whose goalscoring had given them a phenomenal advantage. The Rangers fans were distraught and jeered the team and the club's management. Many felt the decision to sack Scot Symon was a decisive mistake. Celtic won 2-1 in their final game against Dunfermline to finish two points ahead of their old rivals.

As it turned out, the choice of David White as manager was not a success. The younger man – he was just 34 when he took over – lasted for two seasons and became the first Rangers manager not to win a major honour. In 1969/70 he also had the dubious honour of being the first Rangers manager to be officially sacked.

It was tough and frustrating being Rangers during that period in time, for Jock Stein's Celtic were an extraordinary and formidable team with terrifying momentum, one of the best groups of players the United Kingdom has ever produced at a single club.

Rangers would have to wait until 1975 to win the league title again, but in 1972 they did win the European Cup Winners' Cup, beating Dynamo Moscow in the final. Included in their team that evening in Barcelona were Sandy Jardine, John Greig, Willie Mathieson and Willie Johnston, all from the 1968 squad. That, at least, showed the Gers had some very decent teams during Celtic's golden age, but there was a better side in the East End of Glasgow.

In 1968, Rangers' league record was outstanding and in all truth, the real damage was not done at Ibrox Park on 27 April – it had been inflicted at Greenock Morton's Cappielow Park ten days earlier. That 3-3 draw knocked the stuffing out of Rangers and tied one green ribbon around the trophy, but 61 points should have been enough for any team to be champions of Scotland in what was one of the most dramatic title races in Scottish football history. Doubtless, it still rankles with Rangers' long-standing supporters, and the players involved. Rarely have nearly men been so close to triumph.

11

Leeds United 1972:
Trying too hard

LEEDS UNITED won the Football League championship twice under their patriarchal manager, Don Revie, in 1969 and 1974. But in between those title victories they could easily have been crowned champions three times between 1970 and 1972. They were arguably the best team during that period, yet they are equally remembered for being perpetual runners-up and victims of their own high standards.

If fixture congestion had not got the better of them or if they had invested more frequently in their first-team squad, more trophies would surely have ended up at Elland Road. Further proof, if it were needed, of the remarkable drive of this team can be found in the three-year record between 1968/69 and 1971/72; a win rate of 57 per cent, 1.82 goals per game and a points haul of 71 per cent. No other team in the First Division at that time could match that.

Leeds had quite a thin squad, but the first-choice 11 was outstanding. In 1969 their regular line-up included Welsh international goalkeeper Gary Sprake; England caps Paul Reaney, Terry Cooper, Jack Charlton, Norman Hunter and Mick Jones; Scotland's Billy Bremner, Peter Lorimer and Eddie Gray; and Republic of Ireland midfielder Johnny Giles.

Leeds' first championship was the culmination of five years' progress after they were promoted from the Second Division. Revie was appointed manager in March 1961, taking over from Jack Taylor. He was renowned for the so-called 'Revie Plan', a variation on tactics adopted by the Hungarians of 1954, specifically the deep-lying centre-forward.

Leeds were a mediocre outfit at that point and Revie knew the job would not be an easy one. His opening gambit really paved the way for his style of creating the optimal atmosphere within the club, 'It is a challenge, but we will be successful if we all pull together.' The first few months were difficult as Leeds won just one of their last nine games and the following year saw them finish 19th in the Second Division.

Revie's idea was to develop players rather than spend money in the transfer market, and Leeds proved to be very adept at nurturing some bright young talent. In 1962/63, Sprake, Hunter, Reaney and Lorimer started to emerge. Revie had inherited two lynchpins of the team in the form of Bremner and Charlton, both of whom were products of the club's youth team. More came through in the next few years: Paul Madeley, David Harvey, Cooper and Gray.

In 1964, Leeds won promotion to the First Division and they made an immediate impact in 1964/65, although their robust style upset a few people. However, they were very successful and went painfully close to winning the Football League, losing on goal average to Manchester United. Leeds were also chasing the FA Cup and met Liverpool in the final, only to tire and lose 2-1 at Wembley. In many ways it was a foretaste of what was to follow over the next eight years, chasing every trophy, stretching their resources and, ultimately, slipping up in key games. In 1967/68 they were competing on four fronts, but they managed to win their first silverware, the League Cup, beating Arsenal in a bruising final, and the

Inter-Cities Fairs Cup, when they narrowly beat Ferencváros at the start of 1968/69.

Two trophies should have made Leeds and their precocious side relax a little, but it was merely the prelude to the club's first league title win in 1968/69. Leeds, aware that they were not popular, tried to improve their image, but the fact they won more points (67) than scored goals (66) didn't go down well, although it was a sign of the times. They won 27 games and lost just twice, but 15 of their victories were by a one-goal margin.

This was the age of defence-minded football, a British interpretation of the Italian *catenaccio* that had stifled European competition. Revie was fanatical about detail and kept dossiers on rival teams that focused on negating the opposition rather than creating to win. Deep down, though, Revie wanted to build something lasting and memorable, hence he had earlier changed Leeds' colours to all white to ape the mighty Real Madrid.

To some extent he was successful, for plain Leeds became 'super Leeds' and their playing style evolved to make the team one of the most exciting of the 1970s.

In the summer of 1969 Leeds strengthened their team by paying a British record £165,000 to take Leicester City's Allan Clarke to Elland Road. Clarke had only one season with Leicester and was named man of the match in that year's FA Cup Final, which they lost, but they also suffered relegation to the Second Division. Clarke wanted to play First Division football and therefore was keen to move. Although Tottenham and Manchester United were interested, Leeds seemed determined to capture the most sought-after striker in England. They were also keen on Hibernian's Pat Cormack but a move never materialised and he later transferred to Liverpool.

Between 1969/70 and 1971/72, Leeds played some marvellous football. Too often, though, they were exhausted by punishing schedules that were a consequence of continued success. There was criticism that the intensity of Revie's regime also proved too much for mere mortals. Added to this the injuries to vital players at crucial times, such as broken legs for Reaney and Cooper, and it was not hard to feel sometimes that fate was conspiring against Revie and his team.

Certainly there was often a sense of *Schadenfreude* whenever Leeds slipped up, such as in 1970 when they were beaten by a resilient Chelsea in the FA Cup Final after wiping the floor with their opponents at Wembley, or the FA Cup giant-killing at the hands of Colchester United. And then there was the Arsenal comeback of 1971 and the failure at Molineux a year later. Every Leeds setback was amplified and enjoyed by their opponents, but there was also grudging respect for Revie's team, especially in the three-year period when they should have stood astride the game in England.

In 1969/70, Revie promised Leeds would have far more artistic licence and so it proved. Clarke and Mick Jones linked up well from the start and the new man was soon among the goals. Leeds went into 1970 in good form and opened the year with a resounding 5-2 win at Chelsea, who had been in excellent shape. They were also in the last eight of the European Cup and had yet to concede a goal in the competition. The FA Cup had seen them off to a good start, beating Swansea Town, non-league Sutton United, Mansfield Town and Swindon Town. At the end of February they were top of the table, but Everton were two points behind and had a game in hand.

Leeds were closing in on an unprecedented treble of league, FA Cup and European Cup, but the games started to pile up and test their resolve. The FA Cup semi-final with Manchester United was a trilogy that drained the nervous energy of Revie's men. A goal from Bremner took Leeds to Wembley but a two-game saga in Europe, against 1967 European Cup winners Celtic, and a replayed FA Cup Final with Chelsea, broke the backbone of an already over-stretched team. Everton won the league by nine points but most pundits expected Leeds to end the season with some recognition for their efforts. Celtic beat Leeds twice, 1-0 at Elland Road and 2-1 at Hampden Park. This semi-final tie was billed as 'the Battle of Britain', but Leeds were almost running on fumes. 'The elastic has gone,' said one Fleet Street report, with no small amount of sympathy.

In the FA Cup, Leeds were beaten 2-1 by a determined Chelsea in a replayed final after a 2-2 draw at Wembley. Even the most myopic Chelsea fan had to admit that Leeds had been desperately unlucky but as the players sat on the Old Trafford turf, Revie, ever the father figure, picked his lads up and told them to look ahead and start again. 'We've done it before and we can do it now,' he said, while privately admitting he was heartbroken.

Leeds had been criticised 12 months earlier for their style, but in 1969/70 few could complain at the way they played. They scored 84 First Division goals, more than anyone else, including champions Everton who had netted 72.

Leeds provided several players for England's 1970 World Cup squad. Four – Charlton, Cooper, Hunter and Clarke – made the final selection, while Jones was part of the original 40. Reaney was knocked out of contention due to a bad injury and Madeley was added to the expanded squad but opted to stay at home. In short, of Leeds' first-choice team, every eligible member was involved with England at some stage.

Leeds were again contenders in 1970/71 and won their first five games as if they meant to bury the failings of the previous season. Once more, they were aiming at everything: the Inter-Cities Fairs Cup, the First Division and the FA Cup.

But into 1971 they suffered some body blows. First of all they were beaten at home by Liverpool in the league and then a week later, they lost to Colchester in the FA Cup. There was worse to come, although at the beginning of April, Leeds were six points ahead of Arsenal who had three games in hand. Leeds had started to suffer from the two-month absence of Bremner and the prolonged injury to Gray.

While the Gunners kept chipping away at that gap, Leeds drew at Newcastle and then on 17 April came the killer blow. West Bromwich Albion won 2-1 at Elland Road thanks to an offside goal from Jeff Astle that sparked a pitch invasion. Revie was seen walking off the pitch looking to the heavens. 'I have never felt so sick in my life in football, but we shall keep fighting to the last gasp,' he said. Leeds' defeat and an Arsenal win, 1-0 against Newcastle, meant the two teams were level on 58 points, but the Londoners had a better goal average and two games in hand. Losing to West Brom was, in effect, the most crucial defeat of the season for Leeds and the hangover would continue into 1971/72.

They had lost their advantage to an astonishingly dogged Arsenal and as Easter approached, the Gunners were now two points clear. They were then held 2-2 at West Brom while Leeds won 3-0 at Southampton. On 26 April the two teams met at Elland Road and an Arsenal victory would make them champions for the first time since 1953; a Leeds win would keep the issue open for a little longer. It was hard and fast, brutal at times, but with time running out it looked as though Arsenal had done enough to earn a point and edge closer to the title. Then controversy reared its head once more as Charlton, looking offside, scored a scruffy goal to win the contest and keep Leeds' hopes alive.

Before Leeds could complete their league programme, they had to face Liverpool in the second leg of the Fairs Cup semi-final – just two days after beating Arsenal. They drew that 0-0 to claim a place in the final against Juventus. Arsenal had two games remaining, at home to Stoke City and away to Tottenham Hotspur two days after the final round of fixtures. Leeds had just one to play, at home to Nottingham Forest.

Leeds beat Forest 2-0 while Arsenal squeezed home 1-0 against Stoke, which meant the Whites were top with 64 points and Arsenal were a point behind on 63. A point would do for Arsenal, who had a better goal average than Revie's tired team. Ray Kennedy headed a late winner for the Gunners at Spurs to clinch the championship, and Leeds were bridesmaids once more. Revie, gracious in defeat, praised Arsenal's triumphant run, 'We are naturally disappointed having scored 64 points, but we have not lost the title, they [Arsenal] have won it.'

This time there was some consolation in the Fairs Cup, which Leeds won on away goals after drawing 3-3 on aggregate with Juventus. Their final game of a near-300-day season was a 1-1 draw at Elland Road against the Italians, a result that gave them the trophy over the two legs. Over at Highbury, Arsenal were polishing the championship silverware and the FA Cup.

The question was, how would Revie and his backroom team lift a team that must have felt the whole world was against them? The psychological damage done by two seasons of near misses was considerable, but few would ever admit it. Revie would argue that in order to fail, you had to be involved in the latter stages of a competition and that's all his team could do – keep fighting, keep trying and keep together. And nobody could ever deny that Leeds were a tight unit. Team spirit was never a problem and that was down to Revie and his all-consuming approach to building a club. His players loved him and the affection was mutual. They were his lads, hence when he departed in 1974, many found it difficult to function to the same level.

Leeds had to play their opening home games of 1971/72 away from Elland Road, the punishment for the crowd trouble against West Brom in April 1971. This undoubtedly affected their early season form, but they were not the only club who had been forced to play away from their home ground. Manchester United had to play their first two home games at Liverpool and

Stoke after knives were thrown at fans in the away section at Old Trafford during the 1970/71 season. While United picked up maximum points from their travels, Leeds stuttered a bit in the early weeks of the campaign, winning one of their first four and drawing two of their 'home' fixtures at Huddersfield Town and Hull City. They were also beaten 3-0 by newly promoted Sheffield United, after which the local media asked the inevitable questions about the possible decline of Revie's little-changed side.

The Guardian was more forthright, 'These are early days, of course, but not too early to begin to wonder if Leeds United have begun the natural degenerative stage that besets all humans. In a word, are they growing old? The condition is not yet serious, but the weakness of Charlton and Giles suggests that in at least two critical positions Leeds are in need of an elixir or a blood transfusion.'

Certainly, the enforced exile meant it was hard for Leeds to set the early pace. That role went to Sheffield United, who were inspired by players like the headbanded Trevor Hockey, future England star Tony Currie, Stewart Scullion and Alan Woodward.

Leeds regained their mojo and were playing an exciting, more expansive brand of football. There were still occasions, such as in a bruising encounter with old foes Chelsea in London, where they would take no prisoners.

Aware that some of his squad were not as nimble as they had once been, Revie tried to add some younger talent and a midfielder in the shape of Blackpool's Tony Green was on his shopping list. Other players, such as Nottingham Forest's Ian Storey-Moore and Burnley's Steve Kindon, were also linked. After two years of disappointment Leeds needed to bolster their squad, especially after losing one of their key backup men in Terry Hibbitt, who had decided that he was no longer prepared to live off scraps from the top table. Hibbitt, a skilful player, moved to Newcastle United. Goalkeeper David Harvey and England full-back Paul Reaney had also expressed a desire to leave, but both were persuaded to stay.

Revie opted for West Brom's 21-year-old Scottish midfielder Asa Hartford. This took some people by surprise and Revie and his colleagues kept the target a closely guarded secret, securing the deal in a quiet, out-of-the-way cafe. The fee was £170,000 and it was all settled subject to a medical. And that was where the deal fell apart after it was discovered that Hartford had a hole in his heart. He went back to the Midlands; the condition did not prevent the diminutive Hartford from enjoying a full career at club and international level. Arguably Leeds made a big mistake in letting him go so easily, but medical knowledge in 1971 was not as advanced as it is today.

There were echoes of the aborted attempt to sign Alan Ball a few years earlier when Revie could not get approval from the Elland Road suits. Revie later warned the Leeds public that his team needed rebuilding and tried to manage expectations. He spoke of a possible lean period as the club sought out three or four world-class players in their early 20s. Revie's words were quite prophetic, for once the squad started to drift away the club entered an era of steep decline rather than a hiatus.

Leeds in 1971/72, though, were clicking into form, even though their UEFA Cup campaign had ended early in a dramatic collapse at home against Belgium's Lierse SK and their League Cup run was curtailed by West Ham United. It was clear that in 1971/72 they were concentrating their efforts on the league title and the FA Cup.

Leeds ended the calendar year by beating Derby County 3-0 at Elland Road. The fans were chanting 'champions, champions'. The eventual title winners were on the pitch that afternoon, but sadly for Revie it was not Leeds but Brian Clough's Derby, who were challenging the old order as much as the Yorkshire club had a few years earlier. When the two teams met later in the season, the situation would be very different.

Into January, Leeds were closing in on the two Manchester teams at the summit. They overtook United and City at the end of the month but it was a tight race and the lead kept changing hands with Derby, Manchester City, Liverpool and Leeds all in with a shout. In the space of a fortnight, Leeds produced two of their most accomplished performances to remind people they were after the title. First they beat Manchester United 5-1. 'Leeds, in such a mood, could perforate armour plating,' said reporter Tom German. Then came one of the most startling displays over 90 minutes by an English team. Leeds dismantled Southampton 7-0 at Elland Road, displaying all their party pieces, including back flicks, dummies and audacious long passes. They were now favourites for the league but were two points behind Manchester City with two games in hand.

Leeds, never satisfied with going for one gong, were also gathering momentum in the FA Cup. They disposed of Bristol Rovers, Cardiff City and Liverpool before facing Tottenham in the quarter-final. They were in such good form that, after beating Spurs 2-1, pundits and journalists all wondered if Leeds would lose again that season. A mere 17 days later they did just that, a damaging 2-0 defeat at Derby that pushed them into third place behind the home team and Manchester City. The signs were starting to appear once more, and with just one point over Easter after a hard-fought draw at West Ham and that Derby defeat Leeds could be forgiven for believing in déjà vu.

They won through to the FA Cup Final thanks to a 3-0 win against Birmingham City at Hillsborough in the semi-final. Four days later, their title hopes were hit when they lost 1-0 to Newcastle United at St James' Park, the winning goal scored by the brash Malcolm Macdonald.

Leeds were not the only team with the jitters. Manchester City, who had been five points clear at one stage, had seen their title hopes implode after signing Rodney Marsh, a transfer that seemed to upset the balance of their side. On 22 April City beat Derby 2-0, while Leeds won 1-0 at West Brom. City were top with 57 points but had finished their programme. With Liverpool (played 40) and Derby (41) one point behind, and Leeds (40) on 55, City had little chance of finishing ahead of their main rivals.

Liverpool and Leeds were now favourites, but on 1 May, two games took place that would throw more light on the title race – Derby beating Liverpool 1-0 courtesy of a spectacular John McGovern goal and Leeds winning 2-0 against Chelsea at Elland Road. Leeds were now closing in on what they hoped would be the double. They had to face Arsenal on 6 May in the FA Cup Final, and their last league game was two days later against Wolves at Molineux. Liverpool, meanwhile, still had a chance, but had to visit Arsenal on the same night.

Leeds completed the first leg of their double by beating Arsenal 1-0 at Wembley thanks to an Allan Clarke header. The celebrations had to be put on hold as the trip to Wolves at the end of a gruelling schedule was ahead of Revie's side. Derby, meanwhile, had already finished with 58 points from 42 games and were top, and were now sunning themselves in Majorca. If Liverpool won and Leeds failed to get a point at Wolves then Shankly's team would be champions. But if Liverpool only drew and Leeds lost, Clough's holidaying side would win the title. Leeds needed just a single point to win their second league championship. It was, understandably, a tense night in north London and Wolverhampton.

Revie said his team would go all out for victory, 'I reckon it would be soccer suicide to adopt a defensive style of play. Attack is the best form of defence against Wolves. I cannot recall a team being forced to play a championship decider so soon after appearing in a Wembley cup final, but I am convinced there is sufficient character in this Leeds team to accept the challenge and emerge triumphant.'

Revie had asked for the game to be delayed to mid-May, but the Football League wouldn't have it. Not for the first time, Leeds and their fans felt that they were the victims of a conspiracy to make sure their club did not win a major trophy.

It was an evening of drama. Leeds came out full of vigour and had penalty appeals turned down in both halves. In between, Wolves took a first-half lead through Francis Munro and despite pressure from Leeds, they doubled their advantage on 67 minutes when Derek Dougan scored. Billy Bremner pulled one back for the FA Cup winners, but Wolves held on to win 2-1. Over at Highbury, the game between Arsenal and Liverpool ended goalless.

Charlton declared he was 'as sick as a pig' as Leeds trudged out of Molineux. Revie, in his *Yorkshire Evening Post* column, congratulated Derby, but was understandably bitter, 'Deep down, I cannot accept they deserved to snatch the title from Leeds United's grasp. It would be hypocritical for me to say that Derby won the gripping championship race because they were the best side. It was more a case of Leeds failing to get the breaks needed when chasing the elusive double. We have done remarkably well to finish second in the table in view of the setbacks experienced during the last eight months.

'The worst blow, of course, was the [Football] League's decision to force us to play our last league fixture against Wolves just two days after appearing in the FA Cup Final.'

Some questioned if this taxing three-year period had burned Leeds out, and if we had in fact seen the best of this team. But there was still gas in the tank, although in 1972/73 they dropped to third and were beaten in two finals. Then came the second title, which proved to be Revie's swansong, and a European Cup Final in 1975.

Could Leeds have won more? The answer, unequivocally, is yes. Their playing resources were not deep enough, as evidenced when regulars were missing and they called on untried youngsters who had sat watching the first team year-in, year-out. When you're trying to win everything, you need reinforcements and options. Was their approach a contributory factor to repeated shortfalls? Again, the answer has to be yes. Revie's early years made Leeds unpopular with neutrals and this meant opponents raised their game and enjoyed beating them. In some ways, Leeds played 42 cup finals in their league programme every season between 1968 and 1974. Nevertheless, Leeds still won two First Division titles, one FA Cup, two European trophies and a League Cup in a decade. That's a pretty good return by anyone's standards.

12

Poland 1974: No tears
for the clown

WHEN ENGLAND crashed out of the 1974 World Cup at the qualifying group stage, Poland, their conquerors, were seen as also-rans, a relative minnow that had audaciously disposed of the 1966 champions at Wembley.

Yet if the British media had been as informed as they thought they were, they would have realised that this game, which ended 1-1, was almost as significant as Hungary's iconic 1953 triumph. The Poles didn't win, but they were, like the Magyars, reigning Olympic gold medallists. Hungary won the Olympic tournament in 1952, Poland 20 years later. In 1954, Hungary finished runners-up in the World Cup, in 1974, Poland were third. Both teams had other things in common, not least that they were both beaten by West Germany.

In the 1960s and '70s, Polish club football provided some tough opponents in European competition, especially on their own turf. Like many Eastern bloc nations, there was an air of mystery about clubs from Poland, Hungary and East Germany, to name but a few.

Górnik Zabrze, for example, provided Manchester United with a difficult hurdle in the 1967/68 European Cup, with United only narrowly going through on their way to winning the competition. Górnik and Poland had an excellent forward in the form of Włodek Lubański, but he would miss out on his country's finest hour in the World Cup through injury. Lubański was dubbed 'the white Pelé' when his club toured South America. Real Madrid had their eyes on him for some years and once made an audacious US$1m bid to take the player from behind the iron curtain. Ajax, too, in their 1970s pomp, were keen on signing Lubański and apparently tabled a £65,000 bid, but he was prevented from moving abroad by the governing regime.

Poland's resurgence really started in the late 1960s when their club sides started to become more competitive. In 1970 Legia Warsaw reached the semi-finals of the European Cup, losing to eventual winners Feyenoord, and a year later they made the last eight. Górnik were beaten finalists in the European Cup Winners' Cup, losing to Manchester City in a rain-sodden Vienna. As for the national team, in 1970 Kazimierz Górski was appointed as coach. He played just once for Poland in his career, in 1948, but his coaching abilities were never in doubt. He was the master of, to quote the British comedy troupe Monty Python, 'stating the bleeding obvious', making statements like 'in football, you win, lose or draw'.

The fruits of Górski's work started to come to the fore in the 1972 Olympics in West Germany, where Poland played some stunning and very effective football. Poland had not qualified for the final stages of the 1972 European Championship, but the Olympics were seen as an important propaganda opportunity by Polish sports officials, indeed the entire socialist bloc. Although supposedly amateurs, they were far from it in reality as most sportsmen and women were full-time but given roles in the armed forces or other public services.

Poland only just qualified for the Olympics, but once they arrived in West Germany they were exciting and eye-catching. Colombia were beaten 5-1 and Ghana 4-0 in the first two group games, with the Legia Warsaw duo, Robert Gadocha and Kazimierz Deyna, scoring eight of the nine goals.

The third group game was against East Germany, a tough and uncompromising team. Poland had little trouble motivating themselves as the date of the game, 1 September, was the 33rd anniversary of the German invasion of 1939. Poland won 2-1 with Jerzy Gorgoń scoring both goals, sending them into the second stage group with a 100 per cent record.

The next group pitched Poland against Denmark, the USSR and Morocco. The game with the Soviets would be the key after they had drawn with the Danes, and for a long time it looked as though Poland were heading out of the competition. Oleg Blokhin put USSR ahead in the first half and it was not until 11 minutes from time that Deyna levelled from the penalty spot. Three minutes from the end, Zygfryd Szołtysik scored a second to give Poland a 2-1 win. Morocco were then beaten 5-0, but in the process, Antoni Szymanowski was injured and would miss the rest of the tournament.

Poland were in the final, though, and would meet the 1964 and 1968 gold medallists, Hungary. The prospect of two communist states clashing in the final in Munich did nothing to deter the public, who filled the Olympic Stadium to capacity. Hungary took the lead through Béla Varady in the 42nd minute, but by half-time they had lost their leading scorer Antal Dunai, of Újpest Dózsa, to injury.

Poland came back strongly and two goals from Deyna, who was rapidly winning plaudits from the international press, clinched victory. The elegant midfielder scored in the 47th and 68th minutes and was later substituted because of a troublesome groin injury. According to the media, the gold medal had been won by a 'smoothly moving and tremendously impressive Polish side'.

Poland were arguably the best Olympic gold medal winners since Hungary's triumph in Helsinki in 1952, but even then nobody expected them to qualify for the 1974 World Cup as they had England and Wales in their group.

Given it was a three-team group, there was little margin for error. England kicked off in November 1972 in Cardiff against the Welsh in what was Sir Alf Ramsey's 100th game in charge. England were in something of a transition after the failures of 1970 and 1972 and Liverpool's exciting young forward Kevin Keegan was given his first cap. Manchester City's Colin Bell, a member of the 1970 squad, scored the only goal to give the group favourites a scruffy victory.

Wales and England drew at Wembley in the following January and Poland played their first game at the end of March when they were beaten 2-0 by Wales. The key match for the Poles was on 6 June in the heat of Chorzów against England. If they were beaten, it would mean certain elimination, while England needed a confidence-boosting win after a very tepid display against the Welsh. There was an air of tension around England and Ramsey, fairly typically, was very fractious when asked about his team selection. Poland, meanwhile, were awaiting on the fitness of Lubański, who had been kicked above the knee a fortnight earlier and had suffered a setback when receiving another blow that burst his stiches.

The Stadion Ślaski in Chorzów was a vast bowl of intimidating Silesian crowds that made themselves heard for the big internationals. Poland took a seventh-minute lead through Gadocha's free kick that was touched home by a combination of England's Bobby Moore and Jan Banás. It was just the start they needed and the crowd roared their approval. Two minutes after half-time, disaster struck again for the hapless Moore, who made a fundamental error in allowing Lubański the chance to run clear and shoot in off Peter Shilton's left-hand post. Shortly afterwards, Lubański, who had developed a slight limp, was fouled by Derby's Roy McFarland and collapsed. Claims that the Górnik striker was dramatising the situation were unfair, as he was rarely seen in action again over the next couple of years, and Poland's most iconic player was never the same. For England, things just got worse as the game wore on and Alan Ball was sent off in the 76th minute.

Poland's 2-0 win completely changed the dynamic of the group. Wales were now top, England behind on goal difference and the Poles were a point adrift with a game in hand. The emphasis shifted again at the end of September when Poland comprehensively beat Wales 3-0 to send one British team out of the running. Poland went top and put more pressure on England, who had warmed up for the final group game with a 7-0 victory against Austria. While this calmed the nerves of the British press and the England fans, it was also misleading, for Austria were very poor on the night.

Poland needed a point from their final game at Wembley to qualify, whereas England had to win. Ramsey admitted on TV, 'Poland are a better team than most people give them credit for,' but everyone still expected a healthy England win on 17 October. Moore, his career now drawing to a close with both West Ham and England, was dropped and Ramsey filled his side with forwards, but the evening belonged to Poland, despite Brian Clough's insistence that their goalkeeper Jan Tomaszewski was 'a clown'. Clough's comments arguably inspired the ŁKS Łódź man, who saved everything thrown at him. Tomaszewski admitted much later that he had feared a thrashing and was praying to avoid humiliation.

Poland stunned the crowd by taking the lead through Jan Domarski, who shot inside Shilton's post after Norman Hunter, as dependable as Moore once was, slipped up and allowed Gadocha to slide past him. England equalised from the penalty spot through Allan Clarke and then peppered Tomaszewski's goal, but he had the match of his life as he pulled off save after save. It ended 1-1 and Poland were through to West Germany. 'I don't think I have seen a better performance by a visiting country at Wembley,' said Ramsey, who had clearly forgotten about Hungary, Puskás and 1953, a game in which he had played.

Poland had last appeared in the World Cup finals in 1938 when they played one game and were beaten 6-5 by Brazil in Strasbourg. Even though they eliminated England, winners in 1966, at the very ground where they had won the Jules Rimet Trophy, they were not among the favourites in 1974. The draw for WM 74, as it became known in Germany, was on 5 January 1974 in Frankfurt. The bookmakers made Poland 25-1 for the cup, behind Scotland and Chile and nowhere near West Germany, Brazil and Italy. The draw could have been kinder to Poland as it grouped them with Argentina and Italy, both unbeaten in qualifying, as well as unknown makeweights Haiti.

To many people Poland were still unlikely to cause a stir, but by the end of WM 74 Europe knew all about Kazimierz Deyna, Robert Gadocha, Jerzy Gorgoń, Andrzej Szarmach, Władysław Żmuda, Grzegorz Lato and Henryk Kasperczak. It was a rare occasion when a 'golden generation' actually did look special.

The first game, in Stuttgart, saw Argentina needlessly give the ball away to the hungry and fleet-footed Poles, who scored twice in the first eight minutes. In the seventh minute, goalkeeper Daniel Carnevali dropped the ball at the feet of Lato from a corner and the number 16 had the simple task of scoring. Then Szarmach made it 2-0, breaking free and sending a left-footed shot drive past Carnevali. Argentina pulled a goal back on 60 minutes, but Lato took advantage of a poor throw-out by Carnevali to make it 3-1. Babington's scrambled effort reduced the deficit again but Poland were worthy winners.

A 7-0 win against Haiti (who Italy had made hard work of in the first group games) underlined the goalscoring power of Poland, with Szarmach and Lato sharing five goals. Then it was Italy, including Dino Zoff, Sandro Mazzola, Giacinto Facchetti, Fabio Capello and Pietro Anastasi. Poland went 2-0 ahead thanks to a header from Szarmach and a superbly taken first-time shot from Deyna, and future England manager Capello netted five minutes from time for the Italians. There was later talk of an Italian attempt to bribe the Polish players at half-time, but Poland rightfully resisted and sent the *Azzurri* home early, producing 40 penetrative attacks during the game. Poland were the only team to come through their group with a 100 per cent record, and they had scored 12 goals in the process – they were suddenly being taken very seriously.

The next phase of the competition was, unusually, two groups of four. Poland now had to play West Germany, who had conveniently lost to East Germany in the first stage and finished runners-up in their group, while Yugoslavia and Sweden were their other opponents. The other group included the Netherlands, Brazil, Argentina and the East Germans. There were no semi-finals, so Poland had to win the group to go through. The pundits expected their meeting with the host nation on 3 July in Frankfurt would decide one place for the final, with the Netherlands favourites in the other, seemingly tougher group.

People were now talking about Poland as potential world champions and the sceptics who had written them off at Wembley were singing their praises. Brian Glanville, in his book on the World Cup, confessed that had England qualified they would not have made the same impact as the Poles. Regardless of this prediction, Sir Alf Ramsey could at least console himself that England had been eliminated by an excellent team. Even West Germany's Maoist defender, Paul Breitner, admitted Poland were the best outfit in 1974 when looking back on his career: 'I remember one game where I've always maintained we [West Germany] beat a team which was fundamentally better than us. In fact, it was definitely the best team in the competition and still didn't win the World Cup. I mean Poland in 1974.'

Certainly, Poland's forward line had few equals that summer, including Lato, Szarmach and Gadocha. The balding Lato looked older than his 24 years, but his speed and finishing made him one of 1974's most brilliant stars. He played for Stal Mielec, a club from a small town in south-eastern Poland that was synonymous with aircraft manufacturing. Stal were surprise Polish champions in 1972/73, with Lato their leading scorer.

With Lubański unfit, Poland's goalscoring hopes rested with Lato. By the start of the World Cup he had won just 13 caps for his country. His partner up front was 23-year-old Szarmach of Górnik Zabrze, a player who resembled a Gallic cavalier and possessed both pace and rapier-like finishing skills. Both Lato and Szarmach undoubtedly benefitted from the tricky wing play of Legia Warsaw's Gadocha.

The real shining star of Polish football, with the unfortunate demise of Lubański, was Kazimierz Deyna, a tall, dark, angular man with highly artistic feet. Deyna was – on paper – a soldier. His performances in 1974 made him one of the most coveted players in Europe, but the communist regime in Poland prevented him from moving abroad. The list of suitors chasing his signature was astonishing: Real Madrid, Inter, AC Milan, Saint-Étienne, Monaco and Bayern Munich were among the clubs eager for his capture. Deyna had to wait for his chance, by which time he was no longer as fit as he once had been. The Poles were not the only stars coveted by Europe's big clubs, though, for throughout the World Cup there were rumours of deals being discussed for players from both Yugoslavia and East Germany.

Poland faced Sweden in their first last-eight game, a hard-to-beat team who had kept three clean sheets in their opening group, including a goalless draw with the Netherlands. Poland may have been the eye-opener so far in the World Cup but sceptics wondered if their fast, intense style could be maintained for the rest of the competition.

There was no doubt that the contest was getting tighter and more tense and the game with Sweden was settled by a single close-range Lato header. Tomaszewski had to save a penalty by Tapper to ensure Poland picked up two points. West Germany, meanwhile, beat Yugoslavia 2-0 to silence the critics who had been disappointed by the hosts' performances. Four days later, Poland beat Yugoslavia 2-1 with Deyna and Lato on target as they also showed they could defend as well as attack. West Germany won 4-2 against the Swedes, so the decider would indeed come on 3 July.

It was a stormy day in Frankfurt. The skies were apocalyptic, almost Wagnerian. The Waldstadion pitch was sodden, putting the game in doubt between the two best teams in Group B. The kick-off was delayed while the ground staff tried to remove the excess water. It eventually got under way but the surface, as waterlogged as a paddy field, prevented Poland from playing their normal flowing game. Sometimes the ball stopped dead on the puddled pitch; on other occasions it merely skidded. If the game had been played today, it would probably have been abandoned. At the time, former West German skipper Uwe Seeler told TV reporters the pitch was possibly an advantage for the home side, 'This is our weather, a rain-soaked pitch helps our game.'

Surprisingly, it was an entertaining 90 minutes, with both teams going for victory – Poland just had to win, while the Germans could reach the final with a draw. The Poles were without Szarmach, who had been injured earlier in the second round. Sepp Maier, West Germany's imposing goalkeeper, was at his best to prevent Deyna, Lato, Gadocha and Kasperczak from scoring. At the opposite end Uli Hoeneß missed a penalty, his weak effort saved by 'the clown'. With 15 minutes remaining, Rainer Bonhof's run into the area ended with the ball rolling loose to Gerd Müller, who scored with an accurate low shot. It was enough to send West Germany through to the Munich final against the Dutch and end the fairy tale that had been Poland's German summer.

On the eve of the final, the two group runners-up, Poland and Brazil, met in the unwanted third/fourth-place play-off. Lato scored the only goal of a dull and pedestrian match in which Deyna outplayed Rivellino, one of the stars of Mexico '70. This was not Brazil or South America's World Cup – it was very much a European affair.

Poland, along with the Netherlands, had captured the hearts of the neutrals in West Germany. 'A sporting side with attacking ideas and old-fashioned wingers,' said one summary of WM 74. Poland's style wasn't exactly revolutionary, but it was a different approach to many countries who were still absorbed in defence-orientated tactics designed to avoid defeat. West Germany may have ended as champions but the Dutch and Poles were definitely the people's favourites.

As history has told football scholars, the people's favoured teams and inappropriately tagged golden generations are often forced to live with disappointment and the story of 'what might have been'. For example, if Lubański had been fit, would that have altered the outcome, remembering that his replacement and the Golden Boot winner might not have been first choice?

Poland's exciting football had demonstrated that the communist bloc had some outstanding individuals, despite the emphasis on 'the team' and the penchant for function over form. Some opportunists saw eastern Europe as a market for rich pickings, available at a reasonable price, but players were not permitted to leave their home country until they were at an advanced stage of their career. Three of the four socialist states made it through to the last eight, the best showing since the Chilean World Cup of 1962 when Czechoslovakia reached the final.

The Poles were determined to show that 1974 had not been a fluke and were eager to challenge for the 1976 European Championship. The problem was, they had a tough qualifying group that included the Netherlands, Italy and Finland. Poland thrashed the Dutch, including Johan Cruyff, 4-1 in Chorzów in September 1975 with the old guard of Lato, Gadocha and Szarmach scoring the goals. A month later, Cruyff and his team-mates exacted their revenge with a 3-0 victory but it was two 0-0 draws with Italy that really cost Poland and they missed out by a single point.

Two years after finishing third in the World Cup, Poland enjoyed further success in the Olympics. This time it was a silver medal after East Germany beat them 3-1 in the final in Montreal in front of 72,000 people. This game proved to be Gòrski's last in charge of the team as he took up a new position with Greek club Panathinaikos.

The usual suspects were in the Polish side for the Olympics and Szarmach ended as top scorer in a tournament that involved some big future names, including France's Michel Platini, Mexico's Hugo Sànchez, Oleg Blokhin of the USSR and Brazil's Júnior.

Poland eased their way through the 1978 World Cup qualifiers, successfully overcoming the challenge of Portugal, Denmark and Cyprus to book their place for Argentina. They opened the competition with a tame 0-0 draw against West Germany in Buenos Aires but won the group and reached the second stage where they were beaten by both Argentina and Brazil. Their team, the hub of which was largely the same as 1974, was boosted by a few additions, including a young Zbigniew Boniek. They finished third again in 1982. It was a glorious period for Poland and although they have had their heroes since, the team of 1974 is the benchmark every Polish team has to live up to. It has been a tough task.

13

QPR 1976: Total football in the Bush

WEST LONDON belonged to Chelsea between the mid-1960s and early 1970s. Not only were they a vibrant team who could produce stunning football, but they were also trendy and capable of attracting celebrities, actors and even the odd member of the royal family. Chelsea made a lot of noise in that period, casting neighbours Fulham and Queens Park Rangers into the shadows.

QPR started to rise in the 1960s, though, winning promotion from the Third Division to the First Division in consecutive seasons, securing a place in the top flight for the first time in 1968. They also won the first League Cup Final at Wembley in 1967, beating West Bromwich Albion in dramatic style.

In 1967/68, the year that QPR reached the First Division for the first time in their history, Chelsea's attendances at Stamford Bridge were around double their Loftus Road gates. Fulham's crowds were also bigger than QPR's, at an average of 22,000 compared to Rangers' 18,500. Chelsea enjoyed 35,000 crowds at their vast stadium.

QPR's debut season in the First Division was a disaster, failing to win a game until October and ending with just four victories from 42. They went down with only 18 points, using three managers, including former Chelsea boss Tommy Docherty, who lasted for 29 days in the role before falling out with chairman Jim Gregory. The jump from third tier to the top had been too sudden and Rangers didn't have the resources to sustain First Division football.

While Fulham had Johnny Haynes and Chelsea had Peter Osgood, QPR had their own talisman in Rodney Marsh, who eventually left for Manchester City, earning his club a £200,000 fee. Marsh's replacement was, effectively, Stan Bowles, a richly talented player who lived the life of a 'rock and roll' footballer.

After relegation in 1969, Rangers spent four seasons trying to get back to the top. In west London the tide was turning; Chelsea declined significantly between 1971 and 1973, largely because of an expensive new stand, an economic downturn and growing unrest among the players in their relationship with management. There was another side to the story, however, and it forms part of the legend of the club's players of the time. There was a big drinking culture at Chelsea and it is not hard to link that to the declining performance of the team after their FA Cup and European Cup Winners' Cup successes of 1970 and 1971. As Chelsea's star waned, QPR's appeared to be in the ascendancy.

QPR appointed Gordon Jago as caretaker manager in January 1971, a highly respected football man who played for Charlton Athletic and briefly managed the United States national team. Jago replaced Les Allen and had a tough job to lift the mood at Loftus Road, where crowds had dropped to 11,000. Marsh was still at the club and was regaining his best form. QPR ended 1970/71 with just one defeat in ten games so Jago was given the job on a permanent basis.

It wasn't a one-man show, and Marsh wasn't the only player who caught the eye. Jago was assisted by Bobby Campbell and Terry Venables, who was in the team and formulating his own ideas on coaching. Campbell was lured to Arsenal by Bertie Mee, but Venables remained a key figure until he left the club in 1974.

Jago also had some talented young players who could form the nucleus of the team: midfielder Gerry Francis and full-backs Dave Clement and Ian Gillard were all homegrown. Goalkeeper Phil Parkes, a superb, dominant figure, had already been signed from Walsall in June 1970 for £15,000.

In 1971/72, QPR finished fifth in the Second Division, missing out on promotion by two points. Just as they looked as though they were out of the race, Rangers sold Marsh to Manchester City. Marsh was an England international who wanted more caps and felt that playing Second Division football would not help his career. City's Malcolm Allison was always a huge Marsh fan and his team was top of the First Division. 'I am quite certain that some of our supporters will stay away now that Rodney has gone, but most of them will understand we had little alternative,' said Jago as the deal was announced.

While Marsh's arrival at Manchester City seemed to scupper their title hopes, Jago built a better all-round team, using some of the cash received from the sale of their star man. In September 1972, QPR signed Stan Bowles from Carlisle United for £110,000 – a good piece of business for the Cumbrian club as Bowles had been described as a 'scrap-heap player' after being given his cards by Manchester City just two years earlier having made a brief appearance in the club's 1968 title success. He had made a comeback with Crewe and then moved to Carlisle in 1970. The sceptics felt QPR were wasting their money, but Jago was confident he had signed a jewel of a player. 'If Stan Bowles wasn't the right sort of personality for our club, we wouldn't have signed him,' he told the *Daily Mirror*. Without doubt, harnessed properly, Bowles was a ready-made replacement for Marsh.

It was soon very evident that QPR had signed a special player. *The Times* felt that Bowles was a player in the mould of their former striker, 'There is evidence that Marsh may be replaced by another man with something of a rapport with the fans … he has much of Marsh in his movement, much of his control and ability to turn quickly in cramped spaces.'

A month after signing Bowles, Rangers secured the signature of Dave Thomas, a fast winger from fellow promotion-chasers Burnley, for a Second Division record fee of £165,000. Interestingly, just before QPR captured Thomas, Leeds United were apparently lining up a £200,000 bid for the player. Summer arrival Don Givens had cost just £38,000 from Luton Town but ended the 1972/73 season with 26 goals, the Irish striker proving to be a genuine bargain.

Rangers clinched promotion at Cardiff with five games to go. Jago's side had been a joy to watch, playing attacking, thoughtful football. Burnley, who won the Second Division despite losing Thomas, had also been quite progressive in their outlook. The First Division awaited both clubs with interest.

No sooner had the season ended than Jago signed the veteran Arsenal defender Frank McLintock for £25,000 and suggested in the press that the club would spend around £500,000 to ensure they didn't flop like in 1969. But there was a little discontent in the camp as the players refused to accept the new pay deal on offer. Things calmed down and Rangers started the season well, banishing any thoughts of 1969. With Arsenal, Chelsea, Tottenham and West Ham all seemingly declining, QPR found themselves finishing as the top London club in 1973/74.

They repeated the trick in 1974/75, even though they said farewell to Jago, who resigned in October 1974 and moved to Millwall. It was a surprise decision by the popular Jago, but was prompted by a deteriorating relationship with the chairman. Jago described it as the 'most disappointing day of my whole football career'.

Jago left but QPR had an ideal candidate not too far away. Dave Sexton was sacked by Chelsea at the beginning of the month and fitted the bill. He had endured some difficult times at Stamford Bridge which reached a peak with the fall-out with star players Peter Osgood and Alan Hudson. Chelsea backed Sexton at the beginning of 1974, but the club had financial problems and a new stand that had been delayed by a year. Chelsea struggled in 1974/75, eventually getting relegated, by which time Sexton was in his new role.

He enjoyed reminding his old club what they were missing when QPR won 3-0 at Stamford Bridge over the Christmas holiday period, prompting Rangers fans to chant 'Sexton, Sexton'. The balance of power had shifted in west London and Chelsea were about to suffer a slump for the best part of the next decade.

Sexton said on his arrival at Loftus Road that the QPR squad built by Jago was possibly the strongest set of players he had ever inherited as a manager. Rangers did have a very exciting starting 11, but strength in depth was questionable. There was no shortage of experience: McLintock and David Webb at the back had track records and in the summer of 1974, John Hollins was signed from relegated Chelsea, linking up with his old boss.

Sexton was keen to replicate some of the things he had seen in the World Cup in 1974. He had been one of the few managers who went to Germany to discover what made teams like the Netherlands and West Germany tick. Always keen to experiment with continental methods, Sexton had never forgotten the Hungarian team of 1953 and when he saw the likes of Ajax and Bayern Munich, he was excited by the prospect of bringing 'total football' to England. In some ways, Sexton's Chelsea side at the time wasn't ready for some of Sexton's ideas.

The 1974/75 season had been mediocre, but also included a title race that had many contenders. British football was, to some extent, in the doldrums: crowds had slumped, and the England team did not make the last World Cup, Don Revie had taken over as manager, top stars like the Manchester United triumvirate George Best, Bobby Charlton and Denis Law had disappeared and other characters like Bill Shankly and Bill Nicholson had called it a day. The game was looking for inspiration, some brightness in a gloomy landscape. The media liked the look of QPR and so did Revie – he gave their midfielder Gerry Francis his international debut in October 1974 against Czechoslovakia and he was so impressed that within a month of the 1975/76 season's start, he controversially named the 23-year-old as his captain. Francis's England career was brief; he may have been one of the driving forces of QPR's progressive football but he was also injury-prone. By the summer of 1976 his time as England skipper was already over.

QPR couldn't have asked for a tougher start to the 1975/76 season. Liverpool, who had ended 1974/75 without a trophy under their new manager Bob Paisley, brought thousands of fans to London for the start of the season. There was trouble and the travelling supporters gave Francis plenty of abuse in the first half. Rangers were 33-1 for the title, but by the end of the game, that price looked a very good one.

The first goal, scored a minute from half-time, captured much of the spirit of the QPR team. McLintock pushed the ball forward, Bowles played a one-two with Givens and then flicked it square to Francis, who ran on and beat Clemence with a low drive before gesturing to the Liverpool fans.

Mick Leach scored a late second with a brave header,which gave the scoreline some realism. Liverpool were surprisingly tame in defeat, but nobody could deny that QPR's football had lit up the opening day. 'They have forwards with more than one idea, men who improvise in happy harmony like good jazz musicians,' said one report.

A midweek draw at Loftus Road with Aston Villa highlighted that, for all their skilful football, Sexton's men might lack the killer instinct. But at Derby, the reigning champions, QPR capitalised on errors and slack defending to thrash the home side 5-1. Bowles, who was in excellent form, scored a hat-trick on the Baseball Ground's lush new turf. Derby manager Dave Mackay still felt that the game could have ended 4-4, but the scoreline said it all. The result sent some shock waves through English football and confirmed that Rangers had to be taken seriously.

The month ended with two draws, 2-2 at Wolves and 1-1 at home to West Ham, who had started the season well after their FA Cup triumph a few months earlier. Once more, QPR played well, but allowed the visitors to get away with a point. It was a similar story a week later at Birmingham.

The next big test for Sexton's still-unbeaten team was the visit of league leaders Manchester United to Loftus Road on 13 September. The media were delighted that United were back in the First Division after their season away and playing bright, enterprising football under Tommy Docherty, who always provided good copy for journalists. The form of Bowles and Don Masson had attracted the England and Scotland managers, Don Revie and Willie Ormond. Rangers played superbly and took the lead after just three minutes through David Webb. The goal proved to be the winner, but the pundits felt QPR's brilliant team play deserved more reward. 'If Rangers are to sustain their challenge, they must learn to improve and increase their talented approach work,' said one report.

But Rangers were also tight in defence and conceded just six goals in their first ten games, including four consecutive clean sheets. One of those was at Newcastle, where a Mick Leach goal was enough to come away from the north-east with three points. A week later, though, they were beaten for the first time, 2-1 at Leeds. They quickly bounced back with a 5-0 victory against Everton, playing some wonderful football. Even the most hardened sports hack had to concede the standard of football shown by Rangers was some of the best seen in London since Tottenham's hallowed 1961 double winners.

By the end of November, Derby had joined the title race and were reinforced by the signing of Leighton James from Burnley. Stoke City, who had been contenders in 1974/75, were also on the rise. At Loftus Road, Webb scored another vital goal in added time to give Rangers a 3-2 win. Over the next few weeks Rangers seemed to mislay their momentum and lost four games in six. Just before Christmas they were beaten at Liverpool, and they also suffered defeats at Arsenal, Manchester United and West Ham. The sceptics suggested that when the muddy pitches arrived, a team like QPR with their clever, 'touch football' would struggle against old-fashioned English virtues such as hard tackling and brutal challenges. There was no doubt the campaign was going to be tight. By the turn of the year, the leadership had changed 14 times and five clubs had been on top, including Rangers, who had dropped to fifth.

The last of QPR's December and January defeats acted as a springboard for an impressive run that began at Villa Park. While Liverpool and Manchester United were capturing the headlines, Rangers quietly went about their business, winning five consecutive games. Liverpool were now favourites with Derby and Manchester United not too far behind. Rangers were now 9-1 to win the title.

QPR had an advantage over the other challengers in that they had no distractions in their pursuit of the title. Notwithstanding the relatively small size of their squad, they were out of the FA Cup and had no European football, hence they could concentrate 100 per cent on the championship race.

United and Derby were both in the FA Cup (and would meet in the semi-final) and Liverpool had a lengthy UEFA Cup run in progress. West Ham had all but given up at the start of the new year, although they were enjoying a run in the European Cup Winners' Cup.

Rangers had shown they had the durability to last the pace and on 6 March, they returned to the top of the table after beating Coventry 4-1 at home following a very sluggish first half. On the same afternoon, Liverpool, the previous leaders, suffered an unexpected home defeat against Middlesbrough. QPR were two points clear but Liverpool had a game in hand.

QPR travelled to Everton and returned with a 2-0 win thanks to their only shots in the game – 'the height of economy', according to legendary reporter Geoffrey Green. 'Whatever you may think of QPR as a club, they must now be taken seriously by the others as they reach out eagerly for their first championship title in their history,' said Green.

The smart money was starting to be placed on Rangers, who maintained their leadership with two more wins, the second a 1-0 success against Manchester City snatched by yet another vital goal from Webb. Tension was building, though, as the game was a bruiser and included a nasty brawl among the players. Rangers were a point ahead of Manchester United and Derby and two in front of Liverpool, who still had a match to make up.

The title race became a four-horse race before being reduced to two. Manchester United and Derby both lost three of their last half-dozen games, but United beat the Rams to reach their first FA Cup Final since 1963.

Rangers continued winning, disposing of Newcastle at St James' Park and then beating Middlesbrough 4-2 at Loftus Road. Liverpool won the Merseyside derby with a goal from David Fairclough, a player described as 'all legs and carroty hair'. Fairclough became 'super sub', a 19-year-old who had the uncanny knack of scoring vital goals as a 12th man. He would prove to be one of the crucial ingredients in Liverpool's run-in.

The decisive day in the battle for the title was 17 April. Rangers went to Norwich and were beaten 3-2 by a team inspired by the experienced striking duo Phil Boyer and Ted MacDougall. Rangers had won 11 of 12 games and their run had ended at an unlikely place. On the same day, Liverpool beat Stoke City 5-3 at Anfield, taking the Reds to the top of the table and prompting the Kop to claim the championship as theirs. They were one point ahead of Rangers and both had two games to go.

Liverpool had the experience of chasing honours, while Rangers did not. Furthermore, the psychological blow of losing the leadership so late on and also a very impressive unbeaten run was seen as a defining moment in the season. Liverpool had to travel to Maine Road on Easter Monday, on the same day as QPR hosted London rivals Arsenal, who were 17th.

QPR played in the morning and endured a jittery, bad-tempered contest – 'anxiety and frustration walked hand-in-hand' according to the press. Arsenal went ahead but were eventually beat by 2-1 thanks to a disputed penalty from Gerry Francis.

The early kick-off gave Liverpool a distinct advantage and they took the opportunity, winning 3-0 at Manchester City with Fairclough netting twice. 'The ball is very much in our court,' said Bob Paisley after the game.

Quite bizarrely, Liverpool's final match would not be on 24 April, but on 4 May, ten days after QPR completed their campaign. With just one point between them, Liverpool would know exactly what they needed to do and they would be free of the added anxiety of wondering what their rivals were doing. Rangers had to face Leeds at home, but even if they achieved a win and ended their season unbeaten at Loftus Road, they could only wait – and hope.

But Rangers signed off in style against opponents who knew only too well about success and failing at the final hurdle. Leeds had the likes of Billy Bremner, Paul Madeley, Norman Hunter, Joe Jordan and Eddie Gray in their line-up. QPR's refined 'continental' style was a representation of the future, while Leeds were figures from a different era. Dave Sexton always enjoyed a tussle with Leeds under Don Revie when he was manager of Chelsea.

Rangers won 2-0 in front of 31,000 people, the goals coming from David Thomas and Stan Bowles. At the end the fans saluted a fine effort and Sexton and the players returned the compliment from the stand. QPR had gone top by a single point but Liverpool had to play Wolverhampton Wanderers at Molineux on 4 May.

Deep down everyone knew the game was up, that Paisley's Liverpool would have too much for a team struggling to stay in the First Division. Wolves could still stay up but this was a game that had two outcomes in the balance – Liverpool or QPR for the title, Wolves fighting relegation.

The gates at Molineux were closed an hour before kick-off with 51,000 inside the ground. Wolves took the lead after 13 minutes and it wasn't until 14 minutes from time that John Toshack set up Kevin Keegan for the equaliser. The game was settled with two goals in the last five minutes, from Toshack and Ray Kennedy. Liverpool were champions by one point.

The media admitted that while Liverpool had to be respected for their consistency and ability to last the pace, QPR or Manchester United, who had displayed a more inventive and cavalier style, would have been more popular champions. They both won the neutral vote and were greatly admired for the way they played.

Looking back on that wonderful but heartbreaking season for the club, most players have described Sexton's methods as years ahead of their time.

Sadly it was a short-lived moment in the sun for QPR for the 1976/77 season saw them finish in a disappointing 14th. Sexton left the club in 1977 for Manchester United and by 1979, only Ian Gillard was left at Loftus Road of the team that almost became champions. If QPR had succeeded, the future of football in England may have been very different. We shall never know.

14

Netherlands 1978: Déjà vu in Buenos Aires

ONE OF the saddest scenes in 1970s football was the post-match reaction of the Dutch national team on Sunday, 7 July 1974 – vanquished cavaliers walking around the pitch in Munich's iconic Olympiastadion. After enthralling the world in the summer of klaxons and orange-clad fans they were now uninvited guests at a party, golden boys tarnished by unfulfilled expectation. They were supposed to win the competition, destined to provide the crowning moment for 'total football', the mode for a new age.

There was skipper Johan Cruyff, professional but crestfallen, agonisingly encouraging his team-mates to show their appreciation of the crowd, trying to maintain public relations despite an aching heart. The Netherlands were, in many people's eyes, world champions elect, but German efficiency and determination, not to mention Gerd Müller, did for them. As the official FIFA film pointed out, the Dutch were now a team with a great future behind them.

The World Cup hasn't always delivered the best side as champions; witness Austria in 1934, Brazil in 1950 and 1982 and Hungary in 1954. Those who had watched and appreciated the rise of Ajax, Feyenoord and the mighty Cruyff knew 1974 was their time, but equally, some couldn't quite understand how a country that had been a footballing minnow for so long could now be among the favourites for the competition. Things had changed, however, with the coming of professionalism in the Netherlands, and England, for example, had struggled against the Dutch in 1969 and 1970. At the same time, Cruyff had sparkled in 1966 when he tore Liverpool apart in the European Cup, announcing the arrival of their exciting and futuristic brand of football.

The Netherlands played wonderfully for much of the 1974 World Cup, casting aside the South American threat of Uruguay, Argentina and Brazil. The latter victory, a flowing display against a Brazilian team intent on kicking its way to the final, seemed to herald the end of one era and the overture for another. Their big mistake in the final was taking a first-minute lead from the penalty spot through Johan Neeskens, which may have stunned West Germany but also gave them plenty of time to regain their composure, observe their opponents and adapt to the shape of the game. After Paul Breitner had levelled for the Germans with a penalty of their own, Müller put them ahead before half-time with a typical marksman's finish and then the Dutch were chasing the game. There was no doubt the two best teams in the world had met in the final, and the loser would find it hard to take, but you could not help but admire the resolve of the Germans.

Nobody realised during that summer they were seeing Cruyff in a World Cup for the first and last time. As far as most were concerned, at 27 he had at least one more tournament in him, although in some ways 1974 marked the pinnacle and thereafter, Cruyff was never quite the same player.

As many writers have pointed out, Cruyff's fitness, perhaps restrained by his addiction to tobacco, was never as reliable as when he was a young man, and his performances for Barcelona tapered after his initial title-winning season while his influence on the club's future grew.

The 1974 World Cup also saw the end of Rinus Michel's first spell as coach of the Dutch national team. Michels and Cruyff were spiritual partners, both fuelling each other's vision of how football should be played. They had also linked up, briefly, at Barcelona but Michels departed to lead the Dutch to Germany in 1974.

After the defeat in Munich, the Dutch were considered favourites to win the European Championship of 1976. Their qualifying group was exceptionally tough: Poland, who had also delighted in Germany and finished third with a team of fast, attacking players; Italy, who had disappointed in the World Cup but were still Italy; and makeweights Finland. Some experts wondered how Cruyff and others would perform after the devastating loss of the World Cup Final. Would they need motivating and had the team moved beyond its summit? Wim van Hanegem was 30, Cruyff and Robbie Rensenbrink were 27, and at their peak, but others, such as Ruud Krol (25), Johan Neeskens (22), Johnny Rep (22) and Arie Haan (25) had years left.

Cruyff, in his posthumously published biography, said the 1974 World Cup had turned the Dutch team into cult figures around the globe. But the Netherlands without Cruyff were never as compelling, no matter how talented the rest of the squad might have been. He was essential to their pattern of play, leadership, skill and professional mentality. When he departed from Ajax, stung by his team-mates' decision to appoint Piet Keizer as club captain, the Amsterdam club lost direction and confidence. The reign of Ajax that had spanned 1971 to 1973 and three European Cup triumphs was over. Ajax were beaten in the second round of the competition in November 1973 by CSKA Sofia, 2-1 on aggregate, a team they would have overcome comfortably when in their pomp.

Furthermore, Ajax slipped to third place in the Eredivisie, their lowest position since 1965. For three seasons Ajax were pushed into the shadows by PSV Eindhoven and Feyenoord and by the mid-1970s, the golden era of Dutch domestic football was over.

After the 1974 World Cup, Cruyff only really turned out in qualifying games in the European Championship or World Cup. The final in Munich was his 35th cap for the Netherlands, although he went on to make a further 13 appearances before quitting international football, with just two being non-competitive.

The qualifying group for the 1976 European Championship was as tough as predicted. Poland trounced the Dutch 4-1 and Italy beat them 1-0. Away from home they were something of a soft touch, their only victory being a 3-1 success in Finland. At home, they were formidable and they managed to inflict defeats on the Poles and Italians. In the quarter-finals Belgium, their local rivals, were comfortably pushed aside 7-1 on aggregate. The last four also included West Germany, Yugoslavia and Czechoslovakia. Yugoslavia were the hosts and the games were to be played in Zagreb and Belgrade. European football anticipated a re-run of the 1974 World Cup Final, but both the Yugoslavs and Czechs had not read the script.

The Dutch, the firm favourites to win the competition, were their own worst enemies, over-confident and totally focused on who they might meet in the final – in other words, the Germans, whom they yearned to beat to compensate for 1974. They had more or less discounted that Czechoslovakia, their semi-final opponents, would be a formidable hurdle.

The age-old problem of in-fighting and egos hampered the Netherlands in their preparations for the Euros. With Michels gone, their coach was George Knobel, who was never strong enough to deal with the characters and egos in the squad. At one stage, some players left the squad because they were unhappy about the overbearing influence of Cruyff. There were other diva-like incidents that suggested the temperament of the Dutch would ultimately hamper their progress. The latter stages of the 1976 Euros would confirm all was not right.

Instead of strolling into the final, the Netherlands were beaten 3-1 by Czechoslovakia on a wet and windy evening in Zagreb. This was a shock, but the Dutch did themselves no favours in defeat, showing a rather petulant side to their nature. Clive Thomas was the referee and called them 'prima donnas'. The English media felt that the game in Zagreb showed that the Dutch, and Cruyff in particular, had a mistaken sense of superiority. Thomas booked Cruyff in the very first minute of the game.

The Czechs went in front in the 19th minute through a header by their captain, Anton Ondruš, but the same player would score in his own net in spectacular fashion in the 73rd minute to give the Netherlands an equaliser. The Czechs had been reduced to ten men after 51 minutes, but just three minutes after drawing level the Dutch were also a man down after Neeskens was red-carded. The game went into extra time, and six minutes from the end the Dutch were behind once more after Zdeněk Nehoda headed home at the far post. Wim van Hanegem was unhappy and told Thomas, 'No goal – very bad decision.' This resulted in another dismissal and two minutes on, František Veselý rounded Piet Schrijvers to settle the game. The Dutch clinched third place, without Cruyff, thanks to a 3-2 win against Yugoslavia, but once again it was a case of thwarted ambition. After being the golden boys of WM 74, the Dutch attitude to the Euros had somewhat tarnished their reputation.

Cruyff had announced he would retire in 1978 but few people really believed him. He would be just 31 and in theory he had a few more years in him. His fitness had started to wane and his appearances for the national team were coming to an end. Between the semi-final defeat against the Czechs and February 1977 when the Dutch visited Wembley and an out-of-sorts England, he had played just one game.

The reasons for his refusal to travel to Argentina for the World Cup were never fully explained until much later than 1977, but the catalyst was a dreadful incident in his home when armed intruders threatened his family. Cruyff felt he could not travel to Argentina and make his family vulnerable. By the time the World Cup came around, the Barcelona team that included both Neeskens and Cruyff had become unexceptional. In five years at the Camp Nou, Cruyff had won just two trophies with Barca and his goalscoring had only twice reached double figures in La Liga. Furthermore, in his final season with the club, 1977/78, he slipped down the Ballon d'Or rankings from fifth to 15th. But the Dutch team needed Cruyff and the nation refused to give up on him making the trip to South America.

Qualifying for the finals was relatively easy; the Dutch remained unbeaten in six games and conceded only three goals in a group with Belgium, Northern Ireland and Iceland. Their friendly in London was a reminder of what the world would be missing with a Cruyff-less World Cup.

Cruyff was imperious on the night, dictating play, cajoling his team, picking out orange shirts with his pinpoint passing and invention. He touched the ball 61 times (40 more than England debutant Trevor Francis) and of his 50 passes, 30 were positive forward plays. The Netherlands won 2-0 with two goals from Jan Peters, but the 90,000 crowd were treated to a sublime performance from the Dutch master. Such a display only served to underline how important Cruyff would be for the national team. There was no changing his mind, though, and despite campaigns to 'get Johan over the line', the Dutch had to live with the fact that their talisman would not join the bid to win the World Cup.

Knobel lasted until 1976 and was succeeded by army coach Jan Zwartkruis. In 1977 the Dutch football authorities appointed Ernst Happel, the Austrian coach who guided Feyenoord to the European Cup in 1970. Happel's approach was different but had some similarities to the likes of Rinus Michels, although it would seem unlikely that Cruyff and Happel would be natural acolytes given the disciplinarian style of the latter. The relationship between Zwartkruis and Happel was far from harmonious. Nevertheless, Happel was an early adopter of both zonal marking and pressing, which made him a suitable candidate to take the Dutch to Argentina.

With Cruyff out of the picture, there was another blow when Van Hanegem, to many Cruyff's opposite number when the duo were at Feyenoord and Ajax respectively, withdrew from the squad after Happel informed him that he could no longer guarantee him a place in the team. Robbie Rensenbrink, a delightfully skilful player but a shy, reserved fellow, was seen as the key figure who could compensate for the loss of Cruyff. A creative player with an artistic left foot, Rensenbrink started his career at Ajax's city rivals DWS Amsterdam and then spent most of his career in Belgium with Bruges and Anderlecht. His absence from domestic football made him something of an outsider and less familiar with the Ajax/Feyenoord playing systems that dominated the national team, but in 1978, Rensenbrink suddenly became pivotal in his country's World Cup hopes.

The Dutch squad for Argentina included a dozen players from 1974 and a further ten new names. As well as Cruyff and Van Hanegem, goalscorer Ruud Geels had withdrawn and Piet Keizer had retired from international football after feeling slighted over a lack of game time in Germany four years earlier. Younger players such as the 22-year-olds Jan Poortvliet and Ernie Brandts of PSV, and Twente's Piet Wildschut (20) were considered to be part of the future.

The Dutch were drawn in the same group as Peru, Scotland and Iran. On paper it seemed like a comfortable passage but both the Peruvians and Scots were ambitious. Peru still had the brilliant Teófilo Cubillas in their side, a 29-year-old who had made his mark in the 1970 World Cup in Mexico. Scotland travelled to Argentina on the back of a huge promotional campaign and the over-confidence of their manager, Ally MacLeod. In the first group games, Scotland received a rude awakening as they lost 3-1 to a Cubillas-inspired Peruvian side.

The Netherlands, meanwhile, faced Iran in Mendoza and started with nine of the team that kicked off in the 1974 World Cup Final. Iran were heavily motivated with cash bonuses, but they were comfortably beaten 3-0 with all three goals coming from Rensenbrink, two of them from the penalty spot. The Dutch didn't impress on the bumpy playing surface, but they didn't need to be at their very best at this stage.

There were warnings, however, as Peru had clearly been underrated by Scotland and the Scots also made a mess of their second group game, drawing 1-1 with Iran. The Netherlands and Peru met in Mendoza and the game ended goalless. While Scotland were virtually out of the competition, the Dutch still had to clinch their place in the next phase, but if Scotland inflicted upon Happel's team a heavy defeat then a surprise could still take place. For a while, it was a possibility and the Dutch were almost made to regret their somewhat clumsy form in earlier games. Rensenbrink put them ahead with another penalty in the 34th minute but Kenny Dalglish levelled just before half-time. Archie Gemmill sent Scotland in front for the first time at the very start of the second period and then came one of those moments that is forever replayed by TV, a stunning individual goal by Gemmill. Scotland needed another goal to qualify, but their revival was killed by a long-range effort by Johnny Rep. Scotland went home, Peru won the group and the Netherlands had to settle for second place and a berth in the all-European second phase group of West Germany, Italy and Austria. The other group was dominated by South America: Argentina, Brazil, Peru and Poland.

Group A was a tough one. West Germany were a shadow of the 1974 champions although there were few survivors from that team. They had drawn two of their first-phase group games against Poland and Tunisia, but beat Mexico 6-0. Sepp Maier, Berti Vogts and Rainer Bonhof were all involved, as well as Karl-Heinz Rummenigge, a 22-year-old striker for Bayern Munich. Poland were not a surprise package anymore, but they still had a very decent line-up that included Kazimierz Deyna, Grzegorz Lato and new boy Zbigniew Boniek, who would soon grace Italian football. Italy had a squad dominated by Juventus featuring some uncompromising defenders and midfielders such as Gaetano Scirea, Claudio Gentile and Marco Tardelli and a young forward from Vicenza called Paolo Rossi. Italy had exceeded expectations in the first round, winning all three games, including their meeting with hosts Argentina. After a disappointing 1974, Italy had found their form at the right time and were emerging as one of the favourites and the most likely European team to challenge for the trophy. Austria, meanwhile, had also fared better than many felt they would, with their Viennese striker, Hans Krankl, catching the eye.

While Italy and West Germany were drawing 0-0 in the misty Estadio Monumental in Buenos Aires and being jeered off by a critical crowd, the Netherlands finally shrugged aside their lethargy and thrashed Austria 5-1 in Córdoba, an area with a cooler climate that undoubtedly helped the European teams. They went ahead early in the game with a header from Ernie Brandts from Arie Haan's free kick. Rensenbrink netted his customary penalty before Rep scored twice either side of half-time. Erich Obermayer pulled a goal back for Austria but the final word went to Willy van de Kerkhof, who completed the team's return to form.

The second round of matches began to shape the outcome of the World Cup. Italy won 1-0 against Austria with Rossi scoring the winner, while the Netherlands and West Germany met in what would be one of the best games of the competition. The Germans knew that they had to win if they were going to defend their title, but the Dutch would be happy with a draw. On a bright, windswept evening, the two teams rekindled old rivalries and put on a tremendous show for the 40,000 crowd in Córdoba.

Rüdiger Abramczik, the 22-year-old Schalke striker, gave West Germany the lead after just three minutes with a diving, instinctive header after Piet Schrijvers could only parry an edge-of-the-area free kick by Bonhof. The Netherlands' equaliser in the 27th minute was spectacular, Haan's 35-yard shot starting low and rising to a deceptive level to mislead Sepp Maier. The Germans regained the initiative with 20 minutes remaining, Dieter Müller of Köln, the heir to Gerd Müller's throne, sending a downward header past Schrijvers. Helmut Schön's team, who had been low on confidence, suddenly looked more assured with a 2-1 lead to protect.

They did it well up until the 84th minute when Rene van de Kerkhof side-stepped two tackles and curled his shot goalwards, only for defender Rölf Russmànn to dive full length and attempt a last-ditch clearance with his hands. It didn't work and the ball ended up in the net, providing a second equaliser. The Dutch went wild; they might not have won the game but the draw may have eliminated Germany.

The final games saw the meeting of Group A's top two, Netherlands and Italy, while Austria and West Germany were now looking like also-rans. The Italians, arguably the best-balanced team in the competition, dominated and went ahead when Dutch centre-back Ernie Brandts prodded the ball past his own goalkeeper in the 19th minute as he was pressured by Roberto Bettega. Schrijvers was hurt in the incident and had to be replaced by Jan Jongbloed. For much of the first period the Italians were the more accomplished side, but four minutes into the second half Brandts fired a right-footed shot past Italian goalkeeper Dino Zoff from three yards outside the penalty area. Brandts' joyous somersault suggested the Netherlands could sense they were bound for Buenos Aires. Their place in the final was indeed confirmed with 15 minutes to go as Haan sent a blistering long-range shot in off Zoff's left-hand post. Over in the Teutonic derby, Austria pulled off a surprise 3-2 victory against West Germany.

The Dutch, who had arrived in Argentina fractious, homesick and mourning the loss of vital players, had improved as the competition progressed and by disposing of Italy and West Germany they had also demonstrated the power of the team ethic rather than individuals. Their opponents in the final, just as they had been in 1974, were the hosts. Argentina had reached the final by virtue of a controversial 6-0 victory against Peru, giving them the goal difference they needed to finish ahead of Brazil, who had played earlier in the evening.

The build-up for the final, played on 25 June, suggested that Argentina would ride to victory on a wave of emotion, not to mention their high-octane style that was built on speed, aggression and continual movement. But their intense, physically demanding approach was also considered unsustainable by some, so there was an underlying feeling the Dutch method of absorbing pressure, counter-attacking and opportunist shooting from distance could take the trophy back to Europe. Happel's men were also motivated by the prospect of becoming the first European country to win the cup in South America, but they also wanted to show the world they could succeed without Cruyff.

The final was Argentina's moment. Their people, stymied by a dictatorial regime, had provided a fearsome soundtrack, filling stadiums with streamers and ticker-tape. *The Times* summed up that Argentina '78 had provided 'an intense drama set in a theatre of sound and colour'.

The match was long, dramatic and often violent, with the Dutch unwilling to let the hosts play their usual game. Eventually, the constant energy, trickiness and guile of players like Mario Kempes, Leopoldo Luque and Daniel Bertoni proved too much for the Dutch defence. It was the awkwardness of Kempes's long limbs and left foot that effectively decided the final, his two goals a tribute to his determination and somewhat unorthodox style. In fact all three of Argentina's goals, coming after fortunate bounces and destabilising direct runs, were scrappy and could have been avoided. Argentina also adopted gamesmanship to try and unsettle their opponents, notably in keeping the Netherlands waiting for more than five minutes at the start of the match. Then, when they did take the field, they protested about Rene van de Kerkhof's plaster cast on his arm, which had not been a problem until the last minute before kick-off.

The Dutch had plenty of chances in the first half, mostly falling to Rep, who went agonisingly close to giving them the lead. Kempes gave Argentina the upper hand in the 37th minute, receiving the ball from Luque and then prodding his effort under Jongbloed. The Dutch equalised when Dick Naninga headed home a very un-Dutch goal with eight minutes to go. The game headed towards extra time but then came the most dramatic moment of the 90 minutes, Rensenbrink meeting a long pass from Ruud Krol and prodding the ball against the post in a move that almost felt like it was happening in slow motion. Had it gone over the line, the World Cup would have been won and Rensenbrink would have ended the competition as top scorer rather than Kempes.

In extra time, Kempes scored again with another crazy two-step movement and in the dying embers of a fascinating and quite open World Cup, Kempes and Bertoni combined amid the melee of limbs and confetti and Bertoni shot past Jongbloed. The World Cup was won and the Dutch were reluctant bridesmaids once more. It was fair to say that without Kempes the Argentina team would have looked rather plain and somewhat limited, but it was his World Cup.

As for the Dutch, it was now the end of an era. They qualified for the 1980 Euros, the competition's first eight-team tournament, but were way below their best. They were absent from the 1982 World Cup in Spain having performed poorly in a qualifying group comprising Belgium, France, Ireland and Cyprus. Success would eventually come their way in 1988 when Rinus Michels returned as coach to lead a new generation to the European Championship in Germany. The period between 1974 and 1978 was a magical era for the orange shirts, a time when a small European country created a group of highly talented and technical players who went so very close to becoming champions of the world, not once but twice. They might have achieved that remarkable feat in 1978 if Cruyff had travelled.

15

Ipswich Town 1981:
Suffolk comes to the party

FOR A relatively small club, Ipswich Town have played a significant part in football history and have provided two England managers in Alf Ramsey and Bobby Robson. But on the pitch, for a while, Ipswich, a popular, homely club from the east of England, once boasted an exciting team of internationals that deserved greater rewards than just two major trophies. Ultimately, the size of the club proved to be an obstacle difficult to overcome when the pressure built towards the end of a campaign – Ipswich may have had 11 excellent players in 1981, but a lack of depth in their squad prevented them from succeeding on a grander scale.

Before Robson's cultured team threatened to challenge the football hierarchy of the 1970s and early 1980s, Ipswich had won the Football League in 1962, a shock victory if ever there was one, but in a peculiar way the club had a role in the development of England's 1966 World Cup success.

Ramsey's tactics and style, admittedly not the most attractive coda, not only took opponents by surprise but relied on extreme pragmatism and professionalism – it was designed to get results, not quite at all costs, but certainly by making the most of limited resources. While some saw Ipswich as an 'ugly duckling' of a league champion, nobody could deny that in finishing ahead of 1961 double winners Tottenham and an exciting Burnley side they had demonstrated their resilience and commitment.

While Ramsey went on to manage England, Ipswich declined and were relegated in 1964. Their league title success, while remarkable, was dismissed as a one-off. It wasn't until 1968 that they returned to the First Division, this time managed by Bill McGarry. Strangely, McGarry left in November 1968 for Wolverhampton Wanderers, giving up a five-year contract with Ipswich. On virtually the same day, Fulham fired Bobby Robson. Ipswich installed Cyril Lea as caretaker manager but in January they stepped up their search for a new man. Some relatively big names were on Ipswich's shopping list: Frank O'Farrell of Torquay United; Plymouth Argyle's Billy Bingham; and Cardiff City manager Jimmy Scoular, but the Ipswich board had also taken a shine to Robson. He had been helping Dave Sexton at Chelsea with some scouting assignments, but Robson was itching to secure another management position. He was hired by Ipswich on a £5,000-per-year salary, although he didn't have the security of a contract.

Robson, whose playing career included spells with Fulham, West Bromwich Albion and Newcastle United, was an honest broker of a football man who was only 36 years old. He started his Ipswich career well with a draw at a very strong Everton, a 1-0 win at Portman Road over a Manchester United side featuring Best, Law, Charlton et al, and victories against Arsenal, Manchester City and West Ham United. Ipswich's squad was not one designed for the future, however, with their main striker Ray Crawford remaining from their 1962 title win. Crawford was still scoring but moved to Charlton in March 1969.

Ipswich finished 12th, a very respectable position for a promoted team but it wasn't until 1972/73 that they started to seriously make their mark, finishing fourth in the league, their highest placing since the 1962 title win. Furthermore, Ipswich won the Texaco Cup and the FA Youth Cup. That season, they gave a first-team debut to a young centre-back called Kevin Beattie, who made such an impact that pundits were predicting a glittering career among the greats of the game. Unfortunately Beattie became one of football's unluckiest players, crippled by injuries and bad luck.

In 1973/74 Beattie was a key figure as Ipswich finished fourth once more. The team was really shaping up well and although they were some 15 points behind champions Leeds, they were in the ascendancy and among the favourites for honours the following season. Ipswich had an outstanding campaign, starting well and leading the table. The 1974/75 season was a strange affair, with an unlikely set of title contenders: Stoke City, Sheffield United and Middlesbrough all had their moments, while Derby County and Liverpool, who had both won the championship in recent years, were also in the mix. London clubs had declined by 1974 but it was a team from the capital, West Ham, who ended Ipswich's FA Cup hopes in a semi-final replay at Stamford Bridge.

Ipswich faltered in the league, scoring just six goals in their final ten games. Although both Trevor Whymark and David Johnson reached double figures, Ipswich lacked a prolific striker to finish all their fine attacking midfield play. They ended two points off the top, knowing only too well it could have been so much better. They went close again in 1976/77, finishing third behind Liverpool and Manchester City, but by this time Robson had been able to field homegrown talents such as the outstanding John Wark, tenacious Eric Gates and a year later, giant centre-half Terry Butcher. They also signed Paul Mariner, who had made his mark with Plymouth in the Second Division. In 1977/78, despite their league season declining, Ipswich won the FA Cup after beating Arsenal in the final. The images of Bobby Robson dancing in front of huge crowds in Ipswich underlined just how happy a place the Suffolk town was that summer.

Ipswich couldn't compete financially when teams like Nottingham Forest, Tottenham Hotspur and Manchester United were spending big sums, so Robson and his backroom team had to be canny in the transfer market. With the first million-pound player, Trevor Francis, just around the corner, Robson and his employers knew that bargain-hunting would be the club's mantra.

In 1978, English football was still somewhat xenophobic, however, and clubs rarely saw a glimpse of a foreign player. In February 1978 the European Community decreed that the football associations of member states had to allow players from abroad access to England. In the summer of 1978 the Football League lifted a ban that dated back to 1931. Some clubs moved quickly, notably Tottenham, who signed two members of Argentina's victorious World Cup squad: Osvaldo Ardiles and Ricardo Villa. It was more a trickle than a torrent of new talent, but by the end of 1978/79 Ipswich, Southampton, Chelsea, Manchester City and Birmingham City had all signed foreign players.

By sheer virtue of the fact they were 'not from round here', most of these players were popular, their foreign status making them a curiosity. Ipswich acquired two Dutch players, Arnold Mühren and Frans Thijssen, arguably the best overseas duo to enter the Football League in the 1970s. They were more consistent than Spurs' Argentinian pair and helped create a better team than anything that came out of north London during that period.

Robson was looking for something different to make his team into championship contenders. Beattie's fitness had already started to become a concern and Brian Talbot, an industrious midfielder, departed for Arsenal midway through

1978/79. Robson's first venture into the overseas market came in the summer of 1978 when he signed Mühren from Twente for £150,000. Mühren had mixed in good circles, growing up among Ajax's golden generation that included Johan Cruyff. He had won the European Cup in 1973 and was still only 27. His cultured left foot was a joy to watch, although his debut against Liverpool was a setback, a three-goal home defeat. Mühren was anonymous as the game bypassed him, prompting a post-match discussion with Robson. The message was clear, 'I need the ball.'

It wasn't long before Robson started to adapt Ipswich's style and also to take notice of some of the methods adopted by Dutch clubs. Mühren noticed the lack of pre-match preparation, something that was important in his homeland. Pretty soon, his team-mates were warming to pre-match gym sessions and Ipswich became a team moulded in the image of the total footballers from across the English Channel.

Ipswich were still inconsistent and after the Boxing Day draw with Norwich, they were 16th in the First Division and had won just seven of their 21 games. Robson signed Thijssen from Twente for £200,000, providing Mühren with a like-minded partner in midfield. With Thijssen, Mühren and John Wark in midfield, and Mariner, Gates and Clive Woods up front, Ipswich suddenly looked a compelling force that combined traditional English qualities with a touch of the continent.

Their form in the second half of the season was impressive. They lost just twice in 20 games, winning seven of their last eight. They also reached the quarter-final of the FA Cup and were narrowly beaten by Barcelona on away goals in the European Cup Winners' Cup.

The following season, Ipswich were seen as possible title winners, but their start to the campaign was disastrous with Robson's men losing eight of their first 12 games. But after losing to Coventry at the start of December they went 22 games without defeat and finished third, just seven points behind champions Liverpool. By now, Mühren and Thijssen were the driving force of Ipswich's free-flowing style. Robson said of Mühren, 'I cannot think of anyone I would rate higher as a professional. No one worked harder.'

Thijssen, speaking some years later, recalled that when he arrived from Twente, Ipswich played like most other teams, 'The English style was to kick it forward as much as possible, so when you played midfield you had to run forward and if you didn't get the ball, you would have to run back. Bobby [Robson] changed the style, telling the defenders to play it to the Dutch guys in the midfield. That style suited our team very well.'

The 1980/81 season was supposed to be Ipswich's finest hour, but once more the modestly sized club found the pressure of fighting on multiple fronts too much. In some ways, Ipswich had the public's vote thanks to their attractive football along with the fact that against Liverpool, Manchester United and others, they would always be plucky underdogs. British sports fans have always liked the classic struggle of David v Goliath and in this case, Ipswich were cast in the role of David. What's more, Bobby Robson was a popular figure – decent, honest, personable, forthright and seemingly, his ego was well under control. He was the sort of guy you would willingly buy an insurance policy from.

After a few years of consistent performances, which had seen some bright young players emerge, it was only a matter of time before Ipswich would lose some of their crown jewels. With bigger clubs circling Portman Road on a regular basis, if they were going to win big they had to do it soon or risk their team breaking up. Moreover, it wasn't just their players that were coveted by others; Robson himself was in constant demand when a big job was available.

The 1980/81 season provided them with the ideal opportunity, notably when Liverpool, the reigning champions, had a stuttering spell. Their main rivals for the title would be Aston Villa, managed by hardman Ron Saunders and a side who possessed a mixture of flair and honest endeavour. Villa's success was built on a rarely changing team who knew each other well. Brian Clough's Nottingham Forest, champions in 1978, were still around, but lacked the element of surprise that had helped them on their way in their golden period of 1977–80. Forest demonstrated that an unfancied provincial club, with the right management and approach, could win major prizes, even if success could never be enjoyed on the sort of sustainable level more celebrated clubs might expect. Admittedly, they had an extraordinary manager in Clough, but Robson was also seen as a high-quality coach who possessed an uncanny knack of extracting the most out of young players. Ipswich had developed a team that included some of the most sought-after individuals in the Football League and their reputation soon spread beyond British shores.

The 1980/81 season was all about the battle between Ipswich and Villa, with many experts considering the Suffolk side had the upper hand in terms of technique and flair. They started the season well, continuing the momentum of 1979/80, and it was not long before reporters were claiming Ipswich were showing the style of potential champions. After beating Leicester and Brighton, they were held to a draw by Stoke before beating Everton 4-0 at Portman Road. The press were particularly impressed by Ipswich's Anglo-Scottish strike force of Paul Mariner and Alan Brazil, describing the latter as a 'chunky, Scottish action man'.

The top of the table had an unfamiliar look about it, with Ipswich at the summit and a Kevin Keegan-rejuvenated Southampton in second. At the beginning of September, Ipswich hosted Aston Villa and ended the Birmingham side's unbeaten record by defeating them 1-0. Thijssen and Mühren were praised for their 'soothing equanimity' while the robust Brazil was considered to be akin to a 'supercharged tank'. Mariner was 'elegant beyond compare', while Eric Gates had a turn of speed that 'visibly condemns any defender caught too far upfield'.

After a five-game winning streak, Ipswich found themselves four points in front of Liverpool, Everton and Villa. Their next big test was at Anfield, home of the reigning champions. The game ended 1-1, Thijssen scoring a spectacular goal which was cancelled out by a Terry McDermott penalty. Liverpool had not been beaten for more than 70 games at home, so a point was something of a moral victory for Ipswich. Robson was pleased. 'I have said for a while we had felt like a coming team, but now I feel like we have arrived. We can challenge Liverpool for the next few years,' he said.

A draw is a draw is a draw, they say, and Ipswich went through a period of being unable to finish opponents off, against Manchester United, West Bromwich Albion and, on 8 November, at Southampton. The game ended 3-3 and Robson was unhappy at the way Keegan influenced Terry Butcher's sending-off in the 70th minute. Ipswich were without key players for this contest, including Thijssen and Brazil. This string of results cost Ipswich the leadership and they were now second, three points behind Aston Villa who had played 16 times to Ipswich's 14.

Ipswich had already started their European campaign and had worked their way past Aris Salonika and Bohemians Prague. Each time, Ipswich had been impressive at Portman Road with John Wark scoring four times in the first game against Aris, a 5-1 win, and twice in a 3-0 victory against the Czech side. But away from home Ipswich were less confident and solid, losing both times and only just scraping through against Bohemians.

Ipswich lost their unbeaten record, rather surprisingly, away at struggling Brighton. Weakened by injury and suspensions, they were exposed in the air, missing the tall and imposing Butcher and unable to compensate for stand-in goalkeeper Laurie Sivell's lack of height. Brighton scored with less than ten minutes to go and Ipswich were unable to muster up a response. The plethora of draws and their first league loss meant they had won just one in seven.

Wins against Leicester and Nottingham Forest restored normal service and then Ipswich continued their impressive home form in the UEFA Cup, beating Widzew Łódź 5-0 at home. The second leg, while something of a formality, was interesting as Widzew were without three key players – including Zbigniew Boniek – because of an argument at an airport with the national team manager. These were tense times in Poland, and Ipswich were advised not to travel by the Foreign Office. Bobby Robson ignored the recommendation and although his side lost 1-0, they were comfortably through to the last eight.

A draw with Liverpool saw Ipswich play some outstanding football, but the game was slightly marred by some brutal challenges from both teams. Nevertheless, the media crowed about the quality of the two sides in an enthralling 90 minutes. Disaster was ahead for Ipswich, though, as they crashed to defeat at Spurs, conceding five and scoring three. Gates was sent off which meant another suspension. Ipswich were now in third, three points behind leaders Aston Villa, but they had two games in hand.

Ipswich ended 1980 in third but the title race was very tight, with Liverpool and Villa on 34 points, one ahead of Robson's team. Ipswich had played 23 games to the leading pair's 25. If they kept their heads and kept their stars fit, they were in an excellent position to win the title. Or were they?

The FA Cup arrived and the third round paired Ipswich with Aston Villa. It had the potential to be one of the games of the season. Captured in one afternoon, this tie highlighted the differences between the two title contenders: Villa were a team constructed around traditional strengths and the ethos of British football; Ipswich had Thijssen and Mühren, cultured ball players who could elevate them above teams that could run and run. However, there was something more durable about Villa, as the season would reveal as it unfolded. Ipswich won 1-0, Paul Mariner scoring the vital goal.

Meanwhile, in the league, Ipswich embarked on a nine-game run that saw them win eight and draw one. In beating Tottenham 3-0 in the ninth game, Ipswich went a point clear of Villa who had still played one match more. But it was not yet a two-horse race, although Liverpool, Forest and West Bromwich Albion were trailing behind the front-runners. Ipswich's apparent superiority was evident in the Professional Footballers' Association's player of the year voting, which had three of their players vying for top place, John Wark winning the prize with Frans Thijssen and Paul Mariner second and third respectively.

Ipswich had won through to the semi-finals of both the UEFA Cup and the FA Cup. In the FA Cup they had disposed of Shrewsbury Town, Charlton Athletic and Nottingham Forest, the latter after two tight games, including a 3-3 draw at the City Ground.

In Europe they had beaten a talented Saint-Étienne team that included Michel Platini 7-2 on aggregate in the quarter-finals. The remaining schedule for 1980/81 looked intense and Ipswich were starting to tire.

Before facing Manchester United on 21 March at Old Trafford, Ipswich had lost just twice in the league. This game was, however, the beginning of the end as noted by the media who felt the 2-1 defeat suggested there was a chink in their armour. Fortunately for the leaders, though, Aston Villa were beaten at Tottenham.

But in the space of five days, the world changed for Ipswich as they lost two more games and trailed leaders Villa by a point. The two teams had both played 36 times. The second of those defeats, a 3-1 loss at West Brom, saw a depleted Ipswich side lacking their two Dutch masters capitulate rather meekly. Ron Atkinson, the Albion manager, tipped Villa to win the title and felt Robson's men looked as though they were feeling sorry for themselves.

Ipswich won their UEFA Cup semi-final first leg 1-0, thanks to another goal from Wark, but three days later they were surprisingly beaten in the FA Cup semi-final at Villa Park by Manchester City. It was a gruelling afternoon that ran to extra time which may not have been necessary had Ipswich taken some of their early chances. John Bond, the City manager, was a relieved man. 'We know they are a better side than they were today,' he said after the game.

Robson had to lift his team for a return to Villa Park three days later, a game that could decide the outcome of the title race. Ipswich had to win if they wanted to stay in the contest and despite being on the back foot for much of the 90 minutes, they did just that. An early goal by Brazil silenced the Villa Park terraces and in the 80th minute Gates unleashed an unstoppable drive that gave them a 2-0 lead. Only a late effort from Gary Shaw gave Villa hope, but the 2-1 victory had been just what Ipswich needed to lift their sagging spirits.

It was a false dawn, however, for Ipswich then lost two games and all but conceded the title to their rivals. First they lost 2-0 at home to Arsenal, their first defeat at Portman Road all season. They looked completely drained by fatigue and the pressure of chasing glory. Three days later they were beaten 1-0 by Norwich City, a Justin Fashanu goal proving enough to settle the East Anglian derby. Robson admitted afterwards, 'I don't think Villa will hand the title to us now. It looks like second place for us.' Villa had drawn at Stoke but were four points ahead. Ipswich had three games to go, Villa two.

There was still consolation available but Ipswich had to travel to Köln for the second leg of the UEFA Cup semi-final. They won 1-0 to claim a final place against AZ Alkmaar of the Netherlands. Back in the league, Ipswich beat Manchester City 1-0 to give themselves a glimmer of hope. Villa had also won and they remained four points clear.

On 2 May, Ipswich travelled to Middlesbrough while Villa went to Arsenal. Nothing but two victories from their last two games would be enough. Ipswich had a better goal difference by just two goals. The dream lived on, albeit briefly as Villa lost 2-0 at Highbury while Ipswich led at half-time at Ayresome Park. Two goals from Božo Janković gave Middlesbrough a 2-1 win and although Villa lost, they had already done enough to be crowned champions. Ipswich were simply not the same team without their full-strength line-up. Thijssen, for example, missed the last five league games and Ipswich lost four of them.

Thankfully they won the UEFA Cup, beating Alkmaar 5-4 on aggregate after winning 3-0 at Portman Road and losing 4-2 away. They even did that the hard way. A year later they were runners-up again in the league, which proved to be Bobby Robson's last hurrah for Ipswich as he went off to manage England.

As with many clubs who enjoy a golden period, Ipswich could never hope to sustain the success they enjoyed between 1973 and 1981. Two trophies seems a relatively meagre haul when you consider the quality of football they produced and the joy they brought to crowds, but how the Ipswich Town of today would settle for that status.

16

France 1982: *Les Bleus* denied

FRENCH FOOTBALL went back to the top after their national team won the World Cup in 2018, thanks to a glut of highly talented players. But France has always been an influential football country: its administrators were instrumental in the inauguration of the World Cup, the European Championship and the introduction of pan-European club competition. In the 21st century France has a club going head to head with the continent's finest in the form of Paris Saint-Germain. Whatever one's views on the creation of a super club in the city of lights, PSG have helped raise France's footballing profile considerably.

In 1982 France should, at the very least, have reached their first World Cup Final. Footballing folklore insists the moral victors of the competition that year were a Brazil team that, unashamedly, rekindled the flame of Mexico '70, producing the type of football the media and the neutrals always wanted them to deliver on the global stage. But in reality, the team that went closest to providing a people's favourite for the 1982 final was France. Brazil were eliminated in the second phase, failing to make the semi-finals thanks to Italy and Paolo Rossi. France went a stage further and had one foot in the final, eventually losing on penalties to those resilient party-spoilers, West Germany.

France were one of the successors to the total footballers of the early 1970s and in Michel Platini, they had their own Johan Cruyff. After finishing third in the 1958 World Cup in Sweden with a team that included the gifted Raymond Kopa and prolific goalscorer Just Fontaine, France had failed to qualify for 1962, 1970 and 1974. Their club sides had struggled to live up to the exploits of Stade de Reims, who had reached two European Cup finals in 1956 and 1958. Only in 1966 during this period did they grace the World Cup, but even then they came up against hosts England and didn't venture beyond the group stage.

Domestic football took a downturn in France and in 1968/69, for example, crowds for Ligue 1 games slumped to barely 7,000, the lowest post-Second World War average recorded in the French top flight. Something started to change at the start of the 1970s as youth development schemes produced some talented players.

The standard-bearers for French football in the mid-to-late 1970s were Saint-Étienne, a charismatic team who won the hearts of the nation through their big European Cup ties that were screened on television. *Les Verts* were the first French team to benefit from increased broadcasting and their top players soon became household names.

Their coach was Robert Herbin, who was compared to Leeds United's Billy Bremner. Herbin limped from the 1966 World Cup match with England at Wembley after clashing with Nobby Stiles. Influenced by Albert Batteux, the brains behind the Reims side of the 1950s and the France team of 1958, Herbin, in 1972, became one of the youngest coaches in the game at the age of 33.

Herbin's preferred style was not so very different from the approach of neighbouring Holland and Germany. In other words, it was the spirit of total football with *un peu de prudence*. In the European Cup of 1974/75, the continent saw the first signs of an emerging team. *Les Verts* beat Sporting Lisbon, Hajduk Split after a dramatic comeback and Ruch Chorzów on the way to the semi-final, where they met Bayern Munich. Not for the last time, their more flamboyant approach came unstuck against the clinical, methodical and Beckenbauer-organised Germans, who won 2-0 on aggregate.

Saint-Étienne had one of Europe's most promising stars in their ranks in Dominique Rocheteau. He was a 20-year-old forward who had the looks and panache of a teen idol and the sort of virtuosity that earned him the tag of 'the French George Best'. Rocheteau was a graceful player who combined pace, dribbling skills and poise. His nickname was as elegant as his style, *L'Ange Vert*, the Green Angel. He liked rock and roll, notably the Eagles and the sound of west coast America.

Rocheteau was constantly earmarked as a man to watch by publications like *World Soccer* and the 1975/76 campaign saw him come to the fore in the European Cup. Rocheteau and his team-mates won many friends for their performance at Ibrox Park as Saint-Étienne beat Rangers 2-1 to go through 4-1 on aggregate. And then he tore Dynamo Kiev apart as *Les Verts* came back from a 2-0 away defeat to beat the Soviets 3-0. After overcoming PSV Eindhoven in the semi-finals, Saint-Étienne returned to Glasgow to meet old foes Bayern Munich in the final at Hampden Park.

It should have been the crowning of a new European power. Saint-Étienne's flowing football, highly technical and extremely watchable and admirable, made them natural successors to the Dutch masters of Ajax and Feyenoord. Rocheteau could have been almost as influential as Cruyff was for the Netherlands. But there were question marks over his fitness and generally, of Saint-Étienne, stamina – often they would run themselves into the ground. Rocheteau only played seven minutes of the final due to his injury, a familiar tale in his career.

For long periods, Saint-Étienne outplayed Bayern, striking the woodwork and spurning at least a dozen good chances. French fans blamed Hampden's goals for this bad luck, *les poteaux carres*, the square posts. The Glasgow public were willing them on, the watching neutrals urging them to win. But this was Bayern, a team who had soaked up everything that Leeds could muster a year earlier before hitting them with a late double. They had won two successive European Cups prior to this game and knew exactly how to time their run and take advantage of a tiring opponent. It was a free kick from Franz Roth that won the trophy and broke French hearts. For many, it was comparable to West Germany's World Cup win against the Netherlands two years earlier. Tearful Saint-Étienne would never come as close again.

But the renaissance of French club football dovetailed nicely with the rebirth of the national team. In 1978 they qualified for the Argentina-hosted World Cup and appeared to have a team with no small amount of quality, notably in the 22-year-old Michel Platini, the Guadeloupean-born Marius Trésor and, of course, Rocheteau. It was their misfortune to be drawn in one of the first 'groups of death' – hosts Argentina, Italy and a very useful Hungarian side.

This was a World Cup too soon for Platini but having France back in the fold was appropriate given the country's significant role in the creation of football competitions. France were, in many people's eyes, rank outsiders. Their camp was also a little fractious, distracted by commercial issues that upset their idealistic manager, Michel Hidalgo. France started their campaign on fire, taking a first-minute lead in their opening game against Italy, but succumbed 2-1. In their second game they played superbly against Argentina, but found they were not only up against 11 men in blue and white striped shirts but the entire home nation and its fanatic support. Platini, who was tired after a hectic domestic season with Nancy, still caught the eye and equalised after Argentina took a controversial first-half lead but a late winner sent France home early. There were signs, however, that the future looked bright for the French.

Platini, who had complained about a lack of support for his playmaking, was blamed by some French fans for the team's early elimination in Argentina. Throughout the early months of the 1978/79 season he was routinely jeered by fans who felt he had not lived up to his billing as Europe's next big thing. Some years later, Platini recalled his first World Cup as a difficult experience, not least because the Paris intelligentsia, highlighting the South American dictatorship, wanted France to withdraw from the event. Platini, who endured an injury-ravaged season in 1978/79, moved from Nancy when his contract expired, joining Saint-Étienne.

France were expected to qualify for the 1980 European Championship, which was the first to include an eight-team finals in Italy. Their group wasn't an easy one, by any means, including holders Czechoslovakia, the awkward Swedes and little Luxembourg. The French and the Czechs beat each other but France slipped up in their first game, drawing 2-2 with Sweden in Paris. It was a costly mistake and they missed out on qualifying by a single point.

Platini, meanwhile, settled at Saint-Étienne and in his third season he won Ligue 1 while scoring 20 goals. There was to be no European Cup joy, though, for Dynamo Berlin of East Germany knocked *Le Verts* out in the preliminary round. Platini was now in his prime, though, and it was no secret he was going to move in the summer of 1982. Arsenal were very interested but Juventus eventually signed him, paying a nominal fee to Saint-Étienne, a small fortune to the player. Juventus's president at the time, Gianni Agnelli, commented, 'We've paid for a slice of bread and they've given us foie gras!'

The 1982 World Cup was the first to adopt a 24-team format, so there were more places available and from France's qualifying group, a very local affair involving Belgium and the Netherlands as well as Ireland, two spots were up for grabs. The Dutch were no longer the glittering stars of 1974 and 1978 and barely had a member of those two successful World Cups in their ranks. Belgium were stronger and included an outstanding keeper in Jean-Marie Pfaff and extremely dangerous forwards in Erwin Vandenbergh and Jan Ceulemans.

In November 1981, France knocked the Dutch out of contention with a 2-0 win in Paris, but an October defeat in Dublin meant they still had to win against Cyprus to qualify. Belgium had already booked their place for Spain when they beat France 2-0 in the Heysel Stadium a month earlier. France, inevitably, overcame Cyprus 4-0 and edged the Irish out on goal difference. Although making hard work of qualifying, France were still regarded as one of the best European sides to make the finals; in fact many newspapers noted that Michel Hidalgo's team were 'elegant, charming and deadly'.

France's group in Spain included England – happy to be back in the competition for the first time since 1970 – Czechoslovakia and Kuwait. The opener in Bilbao's atmospheric and blisteringly hot San Mamés Stadium paired the French against Ron Greenwood's England, who were without two of their best players in Trevor Brooking and Kevin Keegan, both of whom had stubborn injuries. France had some internal issues as they went into the competition – Jean-François Larios was rumoured to be having an affair with Platini's wife. Larios played in the first game but wasn't seen again until the very end of the competition.

England took a first-minute lead through Bryan Robson, one of the fastest goals in World Cup history. France were shocked by this early setback, but Gérard Soler equalised in the 24th minute and for a while their subtler and smoother skills seemed to suggest they would take control. The heat and humidity were stifling and France began to let the ball do much of the work for them. England were, quite typically, scurrying around furiously, which indicated that they lacked the savvy to progress in a tournament played in an intense Spanish summer.

The determination paid off, though, and in the 67th minute Robson, the best player on the pitch, headed a second for England. Paul Mariner's clincher came in the 83rd minute, by which time both teams were longing for the final whistle. A 3-1 defeat for France was a surprise, but Hidalgo made five changes for the second group game, bringing in Didier Six, Manuel Amoros, Gérard Janvion, Bernard Genghini and Bernard Lacombe to the starting line-up against Kuwait.

In theory, this was the easiest game of the first phase for France but the oil state's representatives had pulled off a 1-1 draw with Czechoslovakia and with the Czechs having lost 2-0 to England, Kuwait still had a chance of progression.

The game was marred by controversy thanks to a bizarre and somewhat comical incident that involving Prince Fahid, the Kuwaiti FA president, concerning a disputed goal. France played superbly and netted through Genghini, Platini and Six in a 17-minute spell either side of half-time. Kuwait couldn't cope with France's energy in Valladolid, although they pulled a goal back. Alain Giresse scored what looked like a perfect fourth goal for France, but the Kuwait team claimed it was offside. Fahid signalled for his players to leave the pitch in protest and then went down to the sidelines and proceeded to argue with the Soviet referee. The goal was eventually disallowed, which incensed the French, but they soon scored another through Maxime Bossis to win 4-1.

England had qualified, but France still had to avoid defeat against Czechoslovakia to secure their place in the next stage, preferably with a win. They also needed a convincing display to demonstrate their credentials. The game ended 1-1, with Six opening the scoring and Antonín Panenka, he of the famous chipped penalty of 1976, netting the equaliser. The Czechs finished with ten men but France were relieved to get off the pitch, even though they had looked in control for most of the 90 minutes. They had qualified, but only just.

This was a strange World Cup in many ways and not one where a single team dominated or played superbly throughout such as in 1970 with Brazil. In the first stage, Brazil had scored ten goals in three games, but the other fancied nations had all stuttered a little. England won all three of their group games, but as the competition progressed they were less and less menacing in front of goal. The second phase, played with four groups of three, paired France with surprise team Northern Ireland and Austria. All the games in that section would be played at Atlético Madrid's Vicente Calderón Stadium.

While some teams had nothing to add to their group-stage performances – England being a case in point – there was always the underlying feeling that France had something in reserve. Aside from Brazil's samba-driven team who had excelled in the tropical heat of Seville, France had the most dynamic midfield, but they had yet to spring into action for a full game. In the second round they raised their standards and improved markedly, largely due to Platini finally finding his very best form and also because winger-turned-centre-forward Rocheteau had returned to fitness after missing two of the three first-phase games.

France beat a stubborn and lethargic Austrian side, which included Hans Krankl and Herbert Prohaska, 1-0 without the injured Platini, thanks to an outstanding strike from free-kick specialist Genghini. Interestingly, some quarters of the press believed that France were a better side without the very individual talent of their captain. Platini's absence, enforced by a leg injury, enabled the diminutive and intelligent Giresse (he was just 5ft 4in tall) to take centre stage and flourish in the role. France played superbly, attacking throughout, and should have won emphatically.

While it was unthinkable that Platini should be excluded from the French line-up, Giresse had certainly caught the eye throughout the competition, so much so that Tottenham Hotspur had decided they wanted the Bordeaux midfielder as a replacement for Osvaldo Ardiles, who had decided the Falklands War had made it impossible for him to return to England. He later changed his mind and Giresse spent his entire career in France, only moving from Bordeaux at the veteran stage of his playing days. Giresse should have been short-listed for the player of the tournament prize, but was seemingly ignored.

France were almost in the last four but had to gain at least a point against media favourites Northern Ireland, who had beaten Spain in the first stage. The Irish knew their fairy tale was coming to a close and manager Billy Bingham was full of admiration for the French side, who he called 'a beautiful team, the best I have seen in the tournament after Brazil'. Before the encounter in Madrid, Bingham felt France had the best midfield quartet and so it proved for Platini, Giresse, Jean Tigana and Genghini wrought havoc for the entire game with their close passing. 'Only Brazil have shown as much imagination,' said one newspaper. At this precise moment, the purists were longing for a France versus Brazil final. Within 24 hours the script would change dramatically and, for some, disappointingly.

France opened up their full box of tricks against Northern Ireland. In the 33rd minute Giresse got the scoring under way after being teed up by Platini. That was the only goal of the first half, but the 37,000 crowd knew more were on their way. Rocheteau, starting for the first time since the England game, scored a second, running half the length of the pitch before beating the veteran Pat Jennings. Rocheteau added a third after

68 minutes before Gerry Armstrong, the hero of the victory against Spain, pulled one back.

Finally, Giresse, the smallest man on the pitch, produced an untypical near-post header to make it 4-1. Northern Ireland's journey was, predictably, at an end, but there was no disgrace to lose to a team full of class and elegance. 'Belfast cries with pride,' claimed the Northern Irish press.

France, though, were now seen as possible champions. A day later, the opportunity seemed to open up as Italy surprisingly knocked Brazil out of the reckoning, Paolo Rossi scoring a memorable hat-trick to send an uninspiring *Azzurri* team through to the semi-final. On the same evening, England drew 0-0 with Spain and sent West Germany through to face Hidalgo's confident team in Seville.

Of the four semi-finalists, only France had captured the imagination of the World Cup public. Italy had laboured in their initial group, drawing all three games, including a 1-1 stalemate with Cameroon. As ever, they had talent, but the fact they recalled Rossi after he was banned from the game demonstrated they lacked options. It proved to be an inspired decision, but Italy were nobody's tip to emerge triumphant. Similarly, West Germany were not the team of 1972 and 1974, but a more mechanical, ruthless version. Poland, although comprising a sprinkling of glitter in the form of Zbigniew Boniek, were not cut of the same cloth as the Deyna team of 1974. The Germans were durable, the Italians had experience. How would France fare against either of these World Cup experts?

Some saw France as the next emerging power, ready to take over at the forefront of European and maybe world football. And with the next European Championship scheduled to take place in France in 1984, the stage was set for a shift.

West Germany, true to form, had recovered from losing 2-1 to Algeria in their first game of the competition and had been rather workmanlike in their path to the semi-finals. They were, after all, the reigning European champions having won a very tepid tournament in Italy in 1980. They had no Beckenbauer or Müller in their squad, but Karl-Heinz Rummenigge of Bayern Munich was their captain and an acceptable heir to the greats of the past. Harald Schumacher, Uli Stielike, Manfred Kaltz, Paul Breitner and Felix Magath were all top performers at various stages of their career. Up front was Horst Hrubesch, a somewhat one-dimensional forward who was, nevertheless, effective, particularly in the air. Hrubesch scored both goals as West Germany beat Belgium 2-1 in the 1980 Euros.

West Germany had been involved in a controversial game against Austria, which they won 1-0, a result that sent both teams safely into the second round. Algeria, who could have gone through if West Germany had scored a second, were incensed, claiming the match had been a conspiracy. There could be no doubt the contest had been a slow-motion affair, devoid of urgency. The neutrals wanted France to beat the West German machine. With Rummenigge consigned to the substitutes' bench due to a hamstring injury, France might have felt their chances had improved, but the Germans took the lead in the 17th minute when Pierre Littbarski, Köln's 22-year-old winger, scored from 18 yards. In the build-up, Rummenigge's replacement Klaus Fischer had bulldozed into France's lightweight and suspect goalkeeper, Jean-Luc Ettori, indicating that West Germany were in the mood for a bruising battle.

France equalised ten minutes later, Platini netting from the penalty spot after Bernd Förster held back Rocheteau. The real talking point of the game, one that is continually raised when the two countries meet, was the aggressive collision involving Schumacher and France's Patrick Battiston. Schumacher came out to meet Battiston, who was heading for goal, but the goalkeeper's crude attempt to stop him resulted in cracked ribs and damaged vertebrae, ending the France substitute's involvement. Schumacher was not even booked for the challenge. The game ended 1-1, forcing the two teams into an extra half an hour in the searing heat of Seville's Estadio Ramón Sánchez Pizjuán.

France scored two spectacular goals in the opening eight minutes of extra time. Firstly, Trésor struck a sublime volley from just outside the penalty area following a free kick. The Germans responded by bringing on a bandaged Rummenigge for Hans-Peter Briegel. Two minutes later, Giresse, 18 yards out, struck a first-time shot in off the post. Surely France were now bound for the final, with just 22 minutes to go?

Rummenigge justified his recall by pulling a goal back and in the 108th minute, Fischer scored with an overhead kick. France were crestfallen and there's no doubt that the blow extended into the penalty shoot-out, a novel way to settle the game. The Germans missed one kick and France two, by Six and Bossis. There was an air of disbelief about the final score as France had been outstanding at times, playing wonderful football. When they led, they simply didn't exploit their advantage.

'We could not defend,' said Hidalgo the morning after. 'My players know only one way, and that is to attack. They are only happy when they are doing that. Now they are shattered, they deserved more than they got last night. Their reward should have been a place in the final.'

Platini, speaking after Hidalgo died in 2020, paid this tribute to his manager, 'As coach, Michel took the France team to its greatest heights, opting for a beautiful style of football which allowed each one of us to fully express our individual talents.'

France versus Brazil. That's what the world wanted. They got it eventually, of course, but not in 1982. Two years later, France, inspired by a peak form Platini, won the European

Championship in Paris with a team that had matured nicely. At least this fine group of players won some acclaim after the heartbreak of 1982, but they could have secured the ultimate crown if justice had been done.

17

Brazil 1982: The last cavaliers

SINCE 21 JUNE 1970, football fans have been urging Brazil to gift the world the essence of samba, the ball-juggling artistry that encapsulated *jogo bonito*, the romantic, natural brilliance that delivers entertainment and excitement. Brazil's 1970 World Cup winners did not represent the start of something; that team was actually the culmination of a process that began amid the despair of Rio de Janeiro 1950. By the time the next World Cup came along, Brazil's 1970 troubadours had mostly gone, with just Piazza, Jairzinho and Rivellino remaining of the all-star XI.

Maybe it was the heat and altitude of Mexico, or perhaps 1970 was a bookend for the crazy and experimental 1960s, but Brazil struggled to replicate the football and the mood of that iconic final at the Estadio Azteca in Mexico City.

In 1974 and 1978 people were generally disappointed by Brazil, a team who had tried, in vain, to ape European methods in order to present a tougher and less vulnerable image to the world. Whatever they were up to, it didn't work, for Brazil were just plain dull in two World Cups, unable to live up to their billing as the great entertainers. Playing 'European' just didn't suit them.

In truth, so many times this has characterised Brazil over the last 50 years. There have been only rare glimpses of the spirit of Copacabana in every finals, but in one of them, 1982, Brazil sent a team out to play and delight and should perhaps have lifted the World Cup instead of Italy. As it happened, Brazil in 1982 merely became another of those 'people's favourites' who fell short of true greatness but whose legend has grown stronger down the decades. This team joined a club that already included Austria 1934, Hungary 1954, Portugal 1966 and Netherlands 1974.

Brazil was under military rule from 1964 to the early 1980s, but the regime gradually fell apart and by 1982 the country was in financial chaos and eventually defaulted on its debt, triggering a deep downturn across South America. By this time Brazil had foreign debt totalling US$87bn, the highest of any country in the world. Football tried to provide some distraction, but politics often encroached on the people's favourite pastime.

In 1980, Telê Santana was appointed as head coach of the national team, a man with a reputation for fair play and who staunchly believed in the traditional Brazilian approach to football. 'Football is art, it's enjoyment and it's not about hoofing the ball upfield,' he would say. History is extremely kind to Santana, largely because he restored some belief in the popular view of Brazil as the footballing equivalent of the Harlem Globetrotters. Not everyone appreciated his style, though, or his stubbornly strict nature. When he took over there was an uncomfortable acclimatisation period that saw him receive jeers and insults from the crowd. But the results spoke for themselves and in more than 30 games, Brazil only lost twice.

Argentina had won the 1978 World Cup on home soil and in the aftermath, they had discovered their new precocious star in Diego Maradona. The 1982 competition was supposed to be his shop window. While the world was getting increasingly fascinated by the Buenos Aires street footballer, Brazil were preparing for the finals, which were to be held in Spain. They had unveiled their 'white Pelé' in 1978, Zico, but he had disappointed in Argentina and was either off his game or injured. Brazil were always uncovering the 'new Pelé' but invariably it didn't work out that way. Zico had the touches, but in a workmanlike and defence-orientated team he couldn't shine. The rest of the world wondered what all the fuss was about over Zico.

The following year, Brazil had the chance to show their fellow South Americans how good they were in the Copa América, but under Cláudio Coutinho they disappointed. Coutinho was militaristic, more about function over form, and he didn't like that most Brazilian of qualities, dribbling. Little wonder he fell out with some of Brazil's more skilful players. After one game in 1978, the fans were so disgruntled with Coutinho's non-Brazilian approach that they burned an effigy of him at a game.

In the Copa América of 1979, Brazil won through their group of three which included Argentina and Bolivia, satisfyingly beating the world champions 2-1 in Rio de Janeiro before 130,000 people. But there was something of a surprise in the semi-finals when they were beaten by Paraguay, who went on to beat Chile in the final.

The World Cup qualifying competition was easily handled by Santana's team, with four straight wins against Venezuela and Bolivia, 11 goals scored, and one conceded. It was the summer tour of 1981 that really acted as a curtain-raiser for the finals and the impressive results prompted the media to pronounce Brazil as favourites for the World Cup. Brazil played three games, against England, France and West Germany – all of whom would appear in Spain – and won them all.

In the build-up to virtually every World Cup, the state of Brazil's team would be the source of great speculation. There was often a degree of kidology involved in order to temper expectation, but as 1981 became 1982 people were talking about the *Seleção* as the best and most exciting since the days of Pelé, Tostao, Jairzinho and Carlos Alberto. Moreover, some critics even went as far as rating the latest team better than the 1970 champions.

Needless to say, in the run-up to the World Cup, discussions over who should make the squad dominated the headlines. Squads were very political in those days and often overshadowed preparations for the competition itself. Luckily, Santana had an embarrassment of riches, notably in midfield.

The squad for Spain included two players who had featured in 1974, goalkeeper Waldir Peres and midfielder Dirceu. Zico was 25 when he became known to the world in 1978, while Cerezo and Oscar had also featured in the squad for Argentina. The public image of the squad was that it was harmonious and 'together', but apparently, there was some friction between the players of Atlético Mineiro and Flamengo. This may have been triggered by the 1981 Copa Libertadores meetings between the two clubs, which both ended in 2-2 draws. A play-off followed and Atlético had five men sent off. Flamengo went on to win the competition for the first time.

The Brazilian squad was evenly spread across the country's domestic game, with Flamengo providing three key players: Zico, Leandro and Júnior. Zico had been named South American Footballer of the Year in 1981, pushing the 1979 and 1980 winner Maradona into second position. While the Argentinian had been getting the headlines and Zico was still relatively unknown outside his native Brazil, the 1982 World Cup was seen as a theatre to provide affirmation for both players. With Zico now 29 years old, it was arguably his last chance to impress the global audience. Before Maradona came along, it was not unreasonable to claim Zico was the best player in the world.

Brazil's captain, and to a large degree, the face of 1982, was not Zico, though. That honour fell to Sócrates, a heavy smoker, a drinker and a bedraggled, messianic figure. Sócrates was political, an outspoken Maoist and the most unlikely looking footballer. But his presence and ability epitomised the team of 1982. He played for Corinthians and specialised in delicate back-heels, as well as radical political statements, including the time he told the people of Brazil that he would never leave the country to play football elsewhere if the government implemented free elections. They didn't and he left, somewhat reluctantly, to play for Fiorentina. He also believed the Brazil team of 1982 was better than the Dutch of 1974, firstly because Brazil had more skilful players and secondly because they did not waste as many chances. 'Our team was the best in the world,' he would say. Ahead of the 1982 World Cup, Sócrates was advised to quit smoking and cut back on beer in order to become even more effective – which seemed to work.

Sócrates and Zico formed part of a sublime midfield quartet that looked as though it was playing for fun. They passed the ball with a touch of fantasy in their boots, finding space and men with accuracy and invention. Falcão was 27 at the time and playing in Italy with Roma. He was a deeply-lying playmaker who combined athleticism and highly refined technique and also had the ability to score spectacular long-range goals. Complementing Falcão was the workhorse of the midfield, the wafer-thin and lanky Toninho Cerezo of Atlético Mineiro. His club team-mate, Éder, although far less industrious, possessed one of the hardest shots in football. He would surely have won more caps had he been more disciplined and cooperative with coaches, but Éder's explosive shooting and spot kicks were still a vital component of the Brazilian team. Similarly, Júnior of Flamengo was a key figure, largely due to his versatility and technique. Instantly recognisable due to his afro hairstyle, he could play on the right or left, in defence or midfield.

Not for the first time, Brazil's team of supreme talents had its soft underbelly. On this occasion it was the goalkeeper, Waldir Peres, who had been included in World Cup squads since 1974. Peres was much-maligned, mostly because of an early mistake in the 1982 finals when he allowed the USSR to take the lead in Brazil's first match. The Brazil side of 1970 was also said to have a weak keeper, but like his predecessors Peres didn't let too many goals in. Similarly, Brazil in 1982 had a less celebrated centre-forward in the form of the muscular and limited Serginho, who still managed to score twice in the competition.

The people of Brazil loved the 1982 team because it revived memories of the fluid, creative style of the past, the approach that had won three World Cups between 1958 and 1970. It included the best player from each of the main football states: Minas Gerais (Cerezo), Rio Grande do Sul (Isidoro), Rio de Janeiro (Zico) and São Paulo (Sócrates). Yet in many ways it was a team for one tournament. Zico was 29, Sócrates, Falcão and Serginho 28, Cerezo, Oscar and Luzinho 27.

Brazil began the group stage with a 2-1 victory against a Soviet team that was good at demonstrating 'less exotic arts'. They took the lead with a long-range effort thanks to a slip-up by Peres. If that confirmed the pre-competition analysis of Brazil's weak spots, the two spectacular goals from Sócrates and Éder that turned the game around rubber-stamped the team as being packed with star quality. 'Brazil were a joy,' said one scribe gleefully after watching their team bring back memories of 1970. Four days later they lined up against a decent Scotland side that employed a massed midfield to counter the threat of Brazil's ball players. In clammy Seville, Scotland had the audacity to take the lead through the sort of goal that Brazil would have been proud of, a fierce, intuitive strike of spectacular design by full-back David Narey. The Scots had, effectively, invited retaliation on a grand scale and it came. Zico netted a delightful free kick that made Alan Rough look like a Highland League keeper, Oscar headed Brazil in front, Éder lifted a spectacular chip over Rough and finally, Falcão shot in off a post. The media were in clover and the World Cup now had its benchmark team.

Brazil had all but qualified for the second phase, so their game against the weakest team in their group, New Zealand, was never going to test them too much. As it happened, the match became something of a showboating exhibition, with Brazil displaying their full array of skills. Zico was in excellent form, netting twice in the first half, one a spectacular bicycle kick, and the second half became a case of how many Brazil wanted to score. Falcão scored a third early in the second half and Serginho added the fourth with 20 minutes to go. As the Samba bands played on, Brazil started to add a touch of carnival to their football, but in truth they should have just continued to score more goals. Often, the desire to produce art did get in the way and a certain casualness would creep in.

The next stage saw Brazil in what everyone popularly called 'the group of death', including an out-of-sorts Argentina who were still preoccupied with the Falklands War and the over-expectation around Maradona, who was looking to move to Europe after the World Cup. And then there was Italy, who had laboured, uninspiringly, through their group with draws against Poland, Peru and Cameroon.

Brazil had charmed their way through the competition, along with a French side who had overcome a defeat in their first game and included the gifted Michel Platini. If football was to be the winner, the final should really have been between these two countries.

Argentina were beaten 2-1 by Italy in the second-stage group of three. The holders now had a very limp grasp on the trophy and their confidence was evaporating with each game. Santana envisaged a tough 90 minutes with their biggest South American rivals and feared some rough-housing. 'We do not want a violent game,' he told the media. 'But we also know that Maradona is not their only star player.' That was very true, but Argentina were not the fast-flowing force of 1978. Mario Kempes, the star of the competition back in Buenos Aires, was slowing and Maradona himself was not in the best frame of mind. Brazil, however, were wallowing in their own self-belief and Zico's reaction in the press said everything: 'We do not play like Italy and Argentina, we enjoy our football.'

Argentina didn't enjoy the clash in Barcelona; Brazil won comfortably and again looked so impressive that pundits declared that for the sake of football, the three-times winners of the World Cup should triumph in 1982. The excitement created by their football and the quality of their goals enthralled everyone, while Argentina looked jaded and seemed very fractious. Brazil took the lead after just 11 minutes when Éder hit a long-range free kick with such venom that Argentina's goalkeeper Ubaldo Filol had no chance to stop the ball. It struck the woodwork, though, and Zico rushed in to push it over the goal line.

Argentina tried to respond but Brazil continued to pepper Filol's goal and it was no shock when they scored twice more, a Serginho header in the 67th minute and Junior's crisp finish after an unstoppable run into the area. Argentina, and particularly Maradona, were frustrated and towards the end, the young player billed as the best in the world boiled over and rather foolishly raised his studs at Batista. Unshaven and looking like a desperate man, Maradona was sent off, despite the appeals of his team-mates. Diaz scored a very late goal, a spectacular effort that was completely overlooked, but Argentina were beaten 3-1 and were out of the World Cup. Cesar Luis Menotti, who had led Argentina to glory in 1978, refused to acknowledge that Brazil had been the better side, but they didn't care too much about sour grapes as they now needed just a point to reach the last four. As for Maradona, his time would come four years later.

Italy, however, had a secret weapon of a sort simmering away in the form of Paolo Rossi, the 25-year-old Juventus striker who had only just returned from a two-year ban due to his involvement in the *Totonero* betting scandal. Rossi, like Italy, had failed to make an impact in the first group stage. Against Argentina, he was subbed for the second time in the competition with ten minutes to go. Rossi's ability prior to his ban was unquestioned, but the decision to take him to Spain was a little controversial. Against Brazil, he would silence the critics and enjoy his finest hour.

Brazil's own talisman, Zico, was doubtful at one point as he was still recovering from Daniel Passarella's harsh challenge on him in the game with Argentina. If he received rough treatment in that match, he was even more intimidated by Italy's formidable defenders.

The encounter would become known as *Tragédia do Sarria*, the tragedy of the Sarria stadium. Rossi opened the scoring after five minutes for Italy with a header on the run from Cabrini's cross to the far post. Sócrates levelled on 12 minutes after a good interchange with Zico, but Rossi made it 2-1 after 25, capitalising on a defensive error by Cerezo. It took Brazil 43 minutes to equalise, Falcão netting with another outstanding goal. At this point Brazil were through to the last four, but they continued to spurn pragmatism and go in pursuit of more goals. With 15 minutes remaining Marco Tardelli played the ball into the area and Rossi turned it home to put Italy ahead and complete his hat-trick. Brazil were behind, and on the brink of elimination. They pressed, they twisted and turned, but the Italian defence refused to yield and prevented Zico from playing his usual game.

At the final whistle there was a sense of disbelief that the overwhelming favourites, the team that had restored faith in the Brazilian ethos of beautiful football, had been knocked out. That 11 never played together again in an international. Most reporters felt the World Cup was going to be poorer for Brazil's failure to reach the semi-finals – and they were not wrong.

Italy and Rossi went on to win the competition, beating a below-par West Germany in the final, and Brazil took the plane home, returning as heroes, despite blowing their chance of glory. An embittered Zico, who would also be named South American Player of the Year in 1982, condemned Italy for not allowing Brazil to play their natural game and commented, 'This was the day football died.' Santana, who remained devoted to his attacking policy, came in for fierce criticism for his naivety in allowing Brazil to expose themselves rather than tighten the team after drawing level for the second time.

In hindsight, it was probably the end of something rather special and unique. Brazil's traditional methods had been beaten by a resilient but rather unexceptional Italian side. Brazilian newspaper *A Gazeta Esportiva* was quite bitter in its assessment, 'Brazil was a light team, a dangerous team that played in pumps. It was a dour, robust, killer team that played in spurs. Brazil played beautifully and mistakenly. Italy played unattractively and assuredly.'

Brazil's last three European competitions had all ended in anti-climax – 1966 in England when Pelé vowed 'never again'; 1974 in West Germany when the Dutch made it clear that football had moved on; and now in Spain when a less-gifted team had deprived them of success. However, the Brazilians of 1982 were not invincible – their style of play, involving deep surges from defence, often left them vulnerable at the back. Most people were blinded to the team's shortcomings due to their brilliance and ability to create the longed-for spectacle.

By the time 1986 came around, Brazil still had some of the '82 squad but they went out of the Mexico-hosted competition in the quarter-finals to France. They were, after all, four years older and past their best. They were still desperate to win the World Cup again and each passing competition would provide a reminder of the gap in time since Brazil were truly Brazil. After analysing where they were going wrong and questioning their own approach, they finally did it in 1994 in the US with a team that had very little in common with the heritage of true Brazilian football. And unsatisfyingly, they did it on penalties after a quite dire game with old foes Italy.

The 1982 team really was the last flicker of romanticised Brazilian football and the eternal flame that was lit as far back as the 1950s, when artistry and guile were staples of their domestic and international game. At the same time, the Brazilians represented the epitome of the free-spirited team, a species that no longer seems to exist in modern football. Such teams are rarely successful in the cynical, hard-nosed game of today – they have too many holes to exploit. Within three years of delighting the world, Têle Santana bemoaned the fact that Brazilian football had become violent and methodical – perhaps a sign that brilliance in failure had run its course?

We still long to be stimulated by superb, raw Brazilian skill, but too often we are let down, even though top footballers are still made and nurtured in South America's biggest nation with alarming regularity. What we are missing today are the animal spirits that gave us Garrincha, Pelé, Jairzinho, Ronaldo, Romário, Sócrates, Falcão, Éder and Zico. Will those days ever truly return?

18

Everton 1986: Heartbreak at the double

EVERTON LOST their way in the 1970s and early 1980s, overshadowed by neighbours Liverpool and unable to stumble upon a settled management team or group of players. Liverpool's success – eight league titles and four European Cups between 1973 and 1984 – was hard to take for a club that had scaled the heights in 1970 with a vibrant team built around the last remnants of the 'school of science' and players like Alan Ball, Colin Harvey and Howard Kendall.

Everton in 1970 averaged 49,000 for their games at Goodison. Only Manchester United drew more people, but by 1983 home attendances averaged just 20,000. Everton, occasionally, would promise to break the malaise, notably in the late 1970s when they attracted some high-profile players, but generally they could only stare across Stanley Park at the silverware parades at Anfield with envy.

In May 1981, Everton appointed Howard Kendall as player-manager. At 35 his playing contribution was limited – just four games – but he had done enough at his previous club, Blackburn Rovers, to suggest he had a promising managerial career ahead of him. Kendall, renowned as one of the best midfielders of his time not to be capped by England, had a hard task to lift the club he graced as a player.

Everton backed Kendall's arrival with transfer funds and they spent in excess of £1.5m on new players. They secured 24-year-old Alan Biley from Derby County, a striker who had made his name with Cambridge United, paying £300,000 for his services. Another £280,000 was paid to Coventry City for Mick Ferguson, a tall forward with considerable aerial prowess. Alan Ainscow, an experienced midfielder, was also signed for £250,000 from Birmingham City.

These players were among a group of signings known as 'the magnificent seven' which also included two goalkeepers, Jim Arnold of Blackburn and Neville Southall from Bury, a centre-back in Bolton Wanderers' Mike Walsh and the Welsh winger Mickey Thomas, who was part of an exchange that saw John Gidman move to Manchester United.

Much was expected of Everton's summer spree, but generally, they disappointed. Only Southall would come through as a long-term acquisition. Biley struggled to adapt on his return to First Division football and by the end of the 1981/82 campaign, he was farmed out on loan to Stoke City. At the same time, Everton signed Adrian Heath, the sought-after 20-year-old Stoke attacking midfielder, for a record fee of £750,000.

Everton finished eighth in 1981/82, an improvement on 1980/81 but still nowhere near to winning major honours. A year later they finished seventh, adding key players including Peter Reid for £60,000 from Bolton, Gary Stevens from their youth system, Kevin Sheedy for £100,000 from Liverpool, and Derek Mountfield for £30,000 from Tranmere Rovers to their squad. Everton's team suddenly had a more youthful look about it, one that was being built with both eyes on the future. In 1983 this strategy was underlined when 20-year-old midfielder Trevor Steven was signed from Burnley for £300,000.

In 1983/84, Kendall's masterplan looked to be heading in the right direction. They added Andy Gray of Wolverhampton Wanderers to their squad in November 1983, paying £250,000 for a player who had cost Wolves a record £1.5m just four years earlier. Everton's league form after Christmas 1983 was outstanding, with just three defeats in 20 games. They also reached the League Cup Final, losing 1-0 to Liverpool in a Maine Road replay after a 0-0 draw at Wembley.

It was in this competition that Everton's turning point came, according to many of their fans. Heath netted a late equaliser at Oxford United in mid-January to earn a 1-1 draw. Everton won the replay easily and began a four-month period that saw them climb the league table and reach two finals.

The League Cup was only half of the story, however, for Everton won through to another Wembley final in the FA Cup and faced Watford. It had been 16 years since their last final, when they were surprisingly beaten by West Bromwich Albion. Kendall was in the Everton side that day and received his second losers' medal four years after his first with Preston North End.

There would be no upset this time as Everton won 2-0 with a controversial headed goal by Gray and a striker's goal by Graeme Sharp. This was merely the prelude to a glorious three-season period when the city of Liverpool could enjoy the success of both of its football giants for the first time since the mid-1960s.

The 1984/85 season proved to be the start of football's rebirth. Sadly, it was hooliganism that triggered it. In May 1985 Liverpool fans were involved in the Heysel Stadium disaster which led to the death of 39 Juventus supporters at the European Cup Final. This terrible evening would have an effect on every club in Britain and would begin a process that would transform football from a declining sport to where it is today. For Everton, the subsequent ban from European competition would prevent an exciting team from fulfilling its potential.

By the time Liverpool met Juventus in Brussels, Everton were league champions by an impressive 13 points, and had also won the European Cup Winners' Cup after beating Rapid Vienna in Rotterdam. They had been beaten 1-0 by Manchester United in the FA Cup Final, falling just short of winning the double. Attendances at Goodison had also increased substantially, their 32,000 average some 66 per cent up on the 1983/84 figures.

The future looked very bright, especially as the average age of Everton's regular line-up was under 24. People started to predict great things and Everton were looking forward to competing in the European Cup, a competition that Liverpool had bossed since the late 1970s. Unfortunately, success was accompanied by outbreaks of hooliganism.

UEFA banned English clubs for one year, initially, and made the penalty indefinite shortly afterwards. With the exception of Liverpool, the ban was lifted in 1990, but in the period 1985 to 1989 Everton and Arsenal both missed out on challenging their title wins.

Everton's successful 1984/85 campaign made them an attractive proposition for potential new players. The season had been a big success from a financial standpoint, with their income of £4.6m higher than that of their neighbours and bettered only by Manchester United in English football. What's more, they had made a profit of almost £340,000 compared to a £175,000 loss in 1984. Philip Carter, the club's chairman, proclaimed 1984/85 to be the club's most successful season in their long history.

Everton made a move for the most coveted striker in English football, Leicester City's Gary Lineker, a fast and goal-hungry player with a good attitude. Manchester United, needless to say, were also interested in the 24-year-old who had netted more than 20 league goals in each of the previous three seasons, forming a lethal partnership with Alan Smith. Lineker had already been capped by England but had yet to make his mark on the international stage. 'We are delighted to have signed him; his record speaks for itself,' said Howard Kendall.

Leicester wanted to fully monetise the deal and were asking £1.25m from Everton, who had bid £400,000. In the end, a tribunal settled on £800,000 and even at that price, the league champions got good value from their acquisition. Lineker's arrival meant the popular Andy Gray, aware that he could quite easily find himself on the fringe of events, moved on and joined his old club Aston Villa. Gray's departure made the job of transition a little harder for Lineker, but as soon as he started scoring goals the doubters were silenced.

Yet Everton had to adapt their style to suit the arrival of Lineker. He was quick off the mark and difficult for defenders to keep pace with, but he didn't have the robust, combative and greatly appreciated style of Gray. Naturally, with the new man's skillset Everton started to hit long balls for Lineker to run on to. This was no attempt at the much-derided Wimbledon or Watford style of play, but it was pragmatic, and it still yielded lots of goals. In Lineker's only season with Everton the team scored 87 league goals, one fewer than in their title-winning year.

Whereas nobody predicted Everton as title contenders in 1984, one year on they were favourites to retain the trophy. English football, though, was under something of a cloud due to the events of May 1985. In a bid to generate more income, a half-hearted 'Super League' was formed among the six clubs that would have played in UEFA's three competitions. Everton would eventually reach the final and play Liverpool over two legs, but nothing could compensate for the loss of potentially lucrative and exciting games in the European Cup.

At the same time, football had a dispute with domestic TV broadcasters and the first half of the season was played without games being screened.

It would, of course, be tough to retain the league, especially as Liverpool were still smarting about a trophyless season in 1984/85 and the fact that English football blamed them for the ban. Everton, ironically, started their defence of the title at Lineker's old club, Leicester. It was one of the surprises of the opening day. Leicester won 3-1 and Lineker's replacement, Mark Bright, who had cost a modest £33,333 a year earlier, stole the show by scoring twice.

Lineker netted his first competitive Everton goal on 26 August at White Hart Lane, a stadium he would grace later in his career. He scored a late diving header to win three points against Tottenham. This victory seemed to inspire Everton, for they clicked into gear with a 4-1 win against Birmingham – Lineker adding a hat-trick – and 5-1 success at Sheffield Wednesday with another two Lineker goals.

Then came a sticky patch of four defeats in nine games, including a Merseyside derby which ended with Liverpool winning 3-2 at Goodison Park. The Reds had gone in at half-time 3-0 ahead but Everton staged a rousing second-half comeback that only just fell short. Kendall's men also seemed to have trouble playing in the capital, losing at Queens Park Rangers, Chelsea and West Ham United, but in November they thrashed Arsenal 6-1 at Goodison. 'It is sometimes alleged that London teams lack the stomach for a fight … Saturday's performance by Arsenal made it seem at least conceivable,' said the Liverpool media.

Everton ended 1985, arguably the best 12-month period they had ever experienced, with three 3-1 wins. They were perched in third place behind Manchester United and Chelsea. While United had started the season in barnstorming style, including a ten-win sequence to open the campaign, they had lost four of their last eight games of the year, including a defeat at Everton. Liverpool were in fourth, largely because they had drawn so many games.

Everton hit the top in early February, taking advantage of Manchester United's ailing form. They went three points clear when they trounced Manchester City 4-0, with the lightning-quick Lineker scoring a hat-trick as he took advantage of some appalling defensive work by City. The fans from Manchester were so impressed, or disillusioned, that they started chanting 'you are the champions' to their hosts. At this stage it did look as though Everton would not be letting go of their trophy in a hurry.

Everton demonstrated their determination when they went to Anfield a week or so later, winning 2-0 thanks to goals from Lineker and Welsh defender Kevin Ratcliffe. The victory maintained a three-point lead over Manchester United and separated the Mersey teams by eight points. Liverpool and Chelsea both had 54 points to Everton's 62 but Chelsea had two games in hand. Chelsea started to fade at Easter when they were beaten 4-0 at home by rising West Ham and 6-0 at Queens Park Rangers in the space of 48 hours.

Meanwhile, Everton were making a gallant attempt to return to Wembley for the third consecutive year in the FA Cup. They had beaten Exeter City, Blackburn Rovers, Luton Town and Tottenham Hotspur to reach the semi-finals where they would meet Sheffield Wednesday.

On 22 March, Everton's 11-game unbeaten run in the league came to an end at Luton, allowing Liverpool – who had regained form and were scoring prolifically – to draw level on points, although the Reds had played one game more. Manchester United were now slipping out of contention.

Everton were now finding goals harder to come by. Over Easter they managed just one, beating Newcastle 1-0 and drawing 0-0 with United at Old Trafford. Liverpool leapfrogged them on Bank Holiday Monday on goal difference.

On 5 April, both Everton and Liverpool won through to Wembley for the first all-Merseyside FA Cup Final, Everton beating Sheffield Wednesday in extra time and Liverpool overcoming Southampton. With both teams also neck-and-neck in the league, the season would effectively be decided in the city of Liverpool. But West Ham had now emerged as serious competitors thanks to a striking partnership of the diminutive Tony Cottee and Scotsman Frank McAvennie.

Liverpool had hit their best form at the right time, improving their goal difference with 5-0 wins against Coventry and Birmingham City. Everton, who were without hamstring injury victim Lineker, ground out wins at Arsenal and Watford, but were fortunate to draw 0-0 with Nottingham Forest at the City Ground. Liverpool were now two points ahead after that emphatic win against Birmingham and the pendulum had swung to the other side of town. It didn't help that Everton had lost their talismanic goalkeeper, Neville Southall, to injury during the run-in. Bobby Mimms, his understudy, took over for the season's climax.

Everton were dealt a severe blow to their hopes at unfancied Oxford United, who had surprisingly won the League Cup. While Liverpool were winning 2-0 at Leicester, Oxford were beating Everton 1-0 at the Manor Ground. West Ham won again and jumped above Everton. Liverpool had 85 points, the Hammers 81 and Everton 80. The title was not beyond Everton, who had two games remaining, but all would depend on how Kenny Dalglish's team fared at Chelsea in their final fixture. If Everton won their two home games and Liverpool lost at Stamford Bridge then they could retain their crown, but two West Ham wins would also make them champions. The first Saturday in May was an exciting afternoon and unlike modern times, it was not manufactured by TV schedules and rearranged fixtures.

What made the finale so different was that Liverpool and Everton were simply the best teams in the land at the time, despite representing a city that had lived through some very tough years in the early 1980s. Fortunately for Liverpool, they were meeting a Chelsea side that had lost the plot after looking so good earlier in the season, but the Londoners still had quality players such as Kerry Dixon and David Speedie, not to mention future Everton winger Pat Nevin. They had won just nine points in their last ten games and they had the look of a team who could not wait for summer to come. Meanwhile, at Goodison, Everton were at home to Southampton and West Ham travelled to relegated West Bromwich Albion.

By half-time Everton were 4-0 ahead against Southampton, with young goalkeeper Keith Granger enduring a nightmare debut for the Saints. Down in London, Dalglish gave Liverpool the lead with a typically well-taken goal. West Ham were in control at The Hawthorns. When full time came, Liverpool had held on to beat Chelsea 1-0 and had clinched the league title. Everton, in rampant form, won 6-1 with Lineker scoring another hat-trick. West Ham won 3-2 but it was to no avail.

Howard Kendall was distraught, but magnanimous, 'I have never felt so low after a 6-1 victory. It was great in the first half when the crowd was roaring, because they had heard, mistakenly, Chelsea had scored. But next Saturday's FA Cup Final is something to look forward to after today.' Dalglish, in the spirit of intense local rivalry, was in no mood to be charitable when asked by the media if he felt for Everton: 'I don't think they would have had any sympathy for us.' Everton ended the season with a 3-1 win against West Ham, securing the runners-up spot.

Amid the conventional local posturing, the city of Liverpool presented a united front to the rest of Britain for the FA Cup Final, even though some Everton fans resented the fact they had been denied a crack at the European Cup because of the behaviour of some of the Reds' fans in Brussels.

Liverpool, for all their success, had only previously won the FA Cup once, in 1965. The two clubs had never met in the final before, but they had faced each other in the semi-finals of 1906, 1949, 1971 and 1977. In both 1984/85 and 1985/86, the two clubs had contested the league title and met in the League Cup Final. They had two of the best goalkeepers around in Bruce Grobbelaar and Neville Southall, the two top strikers in the land in Ian Rush and Gary Lineker, and squads full of young internationals. And both were managed by men who were veritable legends at their respective clubs.

Liverpool had dominated the narrative since the mid-1970s, surviving the loss of Bill Shankly and handing the baton on to Bob Paisley, Joe Fagan and now Dalglish. Everton hoped to succeed their rivals and begin a new era of dominance at Goodison – certainly their fans had suffered enough since Liverpool marched all over English and European football.

After losing the league title from something of a winning position, Everton were keen to level the scores with their old foes. But there was something more at stake – the possibility of winning the double, which in 1986 was a rare achievement. Only four teams had won both the First Division and FA Cup: Preston (1889), Aston Villa (1897), Tottenham (1961) and Arsenal (1971). With a decade of major achievement behind them, Liverpool had never won the double.

Fans from both teams laid siege on Wembley, risking life and limb by climbing over all obstacles. This really was one of those great occasions and the game did not fail to live up to expectations. Everton, clearly motivated, took the lead in the 27th minute, Lineker running on to a through ball by Peter Reid and although his first attempt was parried by Grobbelaar he followed up to score.

Liverpool were frustrated at their lack of progress, Dalglish showing his anger with Kevin Sheedy and Grobbelaar berating his team-mates for sloppy defending. Lineker almost added another goal but Alan Hansen calmly robbed him of the ball. It proved to be a turning point.

In the 56th minute, disaster struck for Everton when Jan Mølby delicately floated the ball into the area and Ian Rush shot home. At that time, Rush's goals meant a Liverpool win and Everton knew it only too well. But Everton almost regained the lead when a bad clearance from Hansen landed invitingly for Graeme Sharp and his header was acrobatically tipped over by Grobbelaar. Liverpool went ahead in the 62nd minute, Mølby sending a low cross towards Dalglish who just failed to connect but Craig Johnston pushed it past Bobby Mimms.

Everton looked finished at this point and suddenly seemed jaded. Mølby was the creator of the third goal by feeding Ronnie Whelan, who picked out Rush on the far side. The finish was perfect from the Welshman and with six minutes remaining, the game was over. After having two trophies within their grasp, Everton were denied twice by the same opponents, who made very clear to the pretender to the throne that they were not going to be pushed into the shadows very easily.

Some people felt Everton were unlucky, as they finished just four points down on their title season and scored one goal fewer. They lost the same number of games and conceded two goals fewer. The two campaigns were almost identical. But they were going head to head with Liverpool, who knew all about winning.

Gary Lineker was sold to Barcelona for £2.8m in the summer, a surprise to many people, but Everton were clearly prepared to let him go. In hindsight, Everton fans have suggested that Lineker didn't totally suit their style of play, that his 40 goals didn't necessarily make them a better team. However, there is also a school of thought that Everton 1985/86 were every bit as exciting as the team that won the championship. In any other season they may well have scooped the lot and 12 months on, they became champions again. But they will never truly know just how good they might have become had they been allowed to compete on the European stage.

19

Hearts 1986: Marooned at the peak

FOOTBALL CAN be a very cruel and unforgiving game, promising everything and delivering nothing. Such is the margin between success and failure that just two goals can change an entire season, break the morale of a team and set it on an instant path of under-achievement. One minute a team can be heroes, the next they're a bunch of failures, consigned to repeat, time and again, that old expression of regret, 'Why?' Heart of Midlothian, a team of young, potential-rich players, went so agonisingly close to winning the Scottish double in 1985/86 but ended with broken dreams and an ache in the midriff that has lasted for decades.

Most of Scottish, indeed British football, grieved for Hearts, who had delighted many people over the course of the campaign, but in the end, they were like the long-distance runner who kept going through sheer instinct, unaware that momentum was gradually ebbing away as they visibly tired by the game, especially as the climax approached. As one pundit said, 'Hearts were almost scared of what they might actually achieve in 1986,' but the truth is, they had a 12-man core squad that rarely got a rest. Eight players made over 30 league appearances from a maximum of 36, and another four well over 20. So many people wanted Hearts to succeed, if only because it represented a challenge to the status quo, but there was a sense of the inevitable about the eventual outcome.

By 1985 Hearts had not won a single trophy since 1960, when they were Scottish champions. In 1965 they almost secured the title but were denied at the death by Kilmarnock, who finished ahead of them on goal average. In 1968 they reached the Scottish Cup Final but were beaten at Hampden Park by Dunfermline Athletic. Sadly, Hearts became better known for their name, their distinctive maroon shirts and their reputation as nearly men than for the silverware they might have won. They had employed some fine players down the decades, though, such as Tommy Walker, Dave Mackay and Alex Young, all of whom enjoyed significant success in England with Chelsea, Tottenham Hotspur and Everton respectively. At the end of the 1970s and into 1980, Hearts found themselves in financial trouble and were close to being placed into receivership.

Scottish football, for a brief period in the early 1980s, became a much more democratic affair, with Aberdeen, Dundee United and then Hearts all becoming more competitive and confronted the so-called 'Old Firm' of Celtic and Rangers. Aberdeen and Dundee United became known as the 'New Firm'.

In 1980 Aberdeen, managed by Alex Ferguson, ended a 14-year run in which the Glasgow duo had won every league title. Three years later, Dundee United won the league for the first and only time in their history. Then Aberdeen were champions in 1984 and 1985. It made Scottish football far more interesting, although it could never be sustained as Celtic and Rangers would always have more power in reserve. By the mid-1980s the pendulum had swung back in the direction of the heavyweights.

In 1984/85 Hearts finished seventh, although there was never any hint that they could mount a serious title challenge.

But they had been on something of an upward trajectory since the arrival of Wallace Mercer as chairman in 1981. Mercer, who was only 34 years old, bought a controlling interest in the club for £265,000 and became one of the great innovators of Scottish football, albeit a controversial and publicity-hungry character who divided opinion.

As well as increasing the club's spending power, despite not being as wealthy as some people liked to believe, Mercer introduced shirt sponsorship to Hearts, CCTV in the stadium, a family enclosure and other improvements. But he went a little too far in some people's eyes when he tried to merge the club with Edinburgh rivals Hibernian. Mercer, who made his money from property development, became public enemy number one in Edinburgh football circles and eventually, the idea of a merger collapsed after anonymous threats were made to the instigators. Mercer's legacy at Hearts was somewhat tarnished by his audacious and ill-timed bid to create an Edinburgh superclub. It was never going to be well received.

Hearts had appointed former Rangers player Alex MacDonald as player-manager in 1981, succeeding Tony Ford, who had a brief spell in charge after former Newcastle skipper Bobby Moncur surprisingly resigned as he was unhappy about boardroom manoeuvring. They were seeking a statement appointment, such as old favourite Dave Mackay, who had a track record with Derby County where he won the Football League in 1975. Hearts were also interested in Jim McLean, the popular manager of Dundee United's 1983 Scottish champions.

The team that went so very close to glory was not expensively assembled by English standards, but transfer fees amounting to £270,000 were paid across several years. The most costly players were Aberdeen-born Andy Watson from Leeds United and 22-year-old John Colquhoun from Celtic, who were bought for £70,000 and £60,000 respectively.

Hearts also signed experience in the form of Sandy Jardine, who was released by Rangers in 1982 after a long and successful career. Jardine had won 38 caps for Scotland and played in the 1974 and 1978 World Cups. He took up a role as Alex MacDonald's right-hand man with the aim of nurturing Hearts' younger players. Hearts fans still credit Jardine with being instrumental in changing the club's fortunes in the mid-1980s, even though MacDonald had been in charge before he arrived.

One of those young players was the highly rated Craig Levein, who was signed from Cowdenbeath for £40,000 in November 1982. At just 19 years of age, Levein was a hot property in the transfer market and had attracted interest from Arsenal, Leeds United and Newcastle United, as well as Rangers, who had been very close to clinching a deal. Levein was named Scottish PFA Young Player of the Year in both 1985 and 1986. Also in defence was Walter Kidd, a tough-tackling right-back who served the club well for 14 years, and Brian Whittaker, a Glasgow lad who had played for Partick Thistle and Celtic. Kenny Black, meanwhile, was a versatile player who could be used at the back or in midfield. He arrived at Tynecastle from Rangers with a £30,000 price tag.

Hearts also developed some of their own talent, notably Gary Mackay and John Robertson, who still hold the club's appearance and goalscoring records. Both made over 500 appearances for Hearts despite being sought after by clubs in Scotland and England. Robertson was reputed to be a closet Hibernian fan but he always denied it as an 'urban myth' that came about because Hibs were desperate to sign him when he was very young, but they could never come to an agreement.

Sandy Clark, a big and uncomplicated forward, had tried his luck in England with West Ham, but returned to Scotland with Rangers and later cost Hearts £45,000. Another key figure up front was John Colquhoun, who joined in 1985 from

Celtic. Hearts had been searching for a winger for a couple of years and MacDonald felt Colquhoun would deepen the squad and prove to be a missing link. MacDonald had also persuaded two of his young players, Levein and Robertson, to remain at Tynecastle, despite tempting offers to leave.

Hearts also benefitted from the steady goalkeeping of Henry Smith, who signed in 1981 from Leeds. Smith was recognised by the international setup relatively late in his career, and but for the likes of Jim Leighton and Andy Goram would surely have won more than his three caps.

Celtic and Aberdeen were seen as probable favourites for the Scottish title, with possible intervention from Dundee United and Rangers. Celtic had players of the calibre of Brian McClair, Mo Johnston, Paul McStay and Tommy Burns, while Aberdeen's big names included Willie Miller, Alex McLeish and Eric Black. The 1985/86 campaign would prove to be Alex Ferguson's last full season with the Dons before he moved to Manchester United. While the media noted that Hearts looked in better shape than their Edinburgh rivals Hibernian, nobody expected them to uproot any trees in 1985/86, especially as they had lost seven of their last nine games at the back end of 1984/85.

It appeared in the early weeks as though the form of the previous spring had carried over into the new season, which did not bode well. Hearts started with a 1-1 draw with Celtic, who only managed to gain a point in added time, but the results continued to go against them, with five defeats in the first eight games.

On a positive note, new signing Colquhoun was in good form, scoring three goals in the first four matches. But defeats at St Mirren (6-2), Rangers (3-1) and Aberdeen (3-0) suggested troubled times lay ahead for Hearts.

By the end of September Hearts had won just once, in the Edinburgh derby, and were sitting eighth in the ten-team

Premier Division. Their fifth defeat in eight was at Clydebank where their team was hit by injuries and was beaten by a very late goal. At this stage, in the days of two points for a victory, Hearts were seven points behind league leaders Celtic.

And then the situation, rather unexpectedly, started to change as Hearts hit upon a rich vein of form. They drew 1-1 with Dundee at Dens Park and then travelled to Celtic, coming away with a stunning 1-0 victory, inflicting the Celts' first defeat of the league campaign. John Robertson scored the winner, receiving a cross from Colquhoun and swivelling to score with a fierce shot. Robertson was later stretchered off, but he had done enough. Celtic were knocked off the top by Aberdeen.

Shortly after that success, Hearts beat Aberdeen 1-0 at Tynecastle, just a few days after the Dons had won the Scottish League Cup. It was a rough contest with lots of bookings, but the game was settled by a dipping header from Levein. This was another impressive win, achieved against a battle-hardened team more accustomed to winning things. It hinted at better times ahead for Hearts after their lacklustre start to the season.

People were starting to take note of the changing mood at Hearts after an impressive 3-0 victory against Rangers in front of 22,000 fans. All three goals came in the second half with Sandy Clark netting twice and Robertson scoring the third a minute from the end. Hearts had climbed the table and were now only five points behind the leaders.

It was Hearts' home form that was really the catalyst for their brilliant revival. When they beat Clydebank 4-1 at a freezing Tynecastle, MacDonald's vibrant team moved into second place in the table, just one point behind Aberdeen. They had now gone nine games without defeat and were unbeaten at home, a record that remained intact for the remainder of the season.

Two more draws, against Dundee and Celtic, extended the run and maintained Hearts' position behind Aberdeen.